STOP CHAS

STOP CHASING WEEKENDS
Find the right work-life balance and win your life back

© 2017 Maja Golob All rights reserved.

Published by:
Spago d.o.o., Hotična 2a, 6242 Materija, www.spago.si, info@spago.si
Hotična, 2017
Contact: Aco Spasović

For more information please visit: www.stopchasingweekends.com or write to info@stopchasingweekends.com

Translation: Maja Golob
Proofreading: Murray Bales, Natalie Margaret Nicholls
Design: Spago d.o.o., Studio Aleja d.o.o., Designlicious Kristina Smodila
Illustrations: Shutterstock and Sonja Eržen
Cover photo: Manca Birk Photography
Format: Paperback; 5,5" x 8,5" (13,97 cm x 21,59 cm)
Available at: amazon.com

CIP - Kataložni zapis o publikaciji
Narodna in univerzitetna knjižnica, Ljubljana

159.922(035)
316.728(035)
379.82(035)
159.937.53:316.728

GOLOB, Maja, 1971-
    Stop chasing weekends : find the right work-life balance and win back your life / [text, translation] Maja Golob ; [illustrations Shutterstock and Sonja Eržen]. - Hotična : Spago, 2017

ISBN 978-961-94180-0-0

289120512

Maja Golob

STOP CHASING WEEKENDS

———

Find the right work-life balance
and win your life back

READER **REVIEWS**

"I loved it! I sincerely hope women will find a ray of light within it and transform it into their own light, one that leads to happiness. Thank you for sharing your story with the world!"

IZA LOGIN, Cyprus

"Like the intimate confession of a friend, yet so much more, as it warmly empowers the reader to develop their inner strength and follow their personal mission."

SONJA KLOPČIČ, entrepreneur, manager, leader and author of The Energy Inside Leadership, Slovenia

"I am grateful for the very clear reminder that crafting our life is both a choice and an art. An art that is sometimes shaped by difficult experiences and sad events. Thank you Maja!"

LETIZIA ACCINELLI, Member of the Nia Training Faculty, Nia White Belt Trainer, Italy

"This is an optimistic and inspiring book you will not want to put down until it is finished!"

NIVES MAHNE ČEHOVIN, mother, wife and entrepreneur, Slovenia

Stop chasing weekends

"The lessons Maja highlights throughout her book really made me think about myself – if I want to be truly fulfilled, I need to take care of myself first. A must-read for any woman who wants to take back her true girl power."

NATALIE MARGARET NICHOLLS, a mum to 3 boys, a wife and entrepreneur, United Kingdom

———

"Maja helps the reader focus their mind on a single goal: to find their own path to inner peace and happiness. The author says this book is for women only, but I say it's universal and timeless."

BARBARA MODIC, Managing Director of Pristop Media, Slovenia

———

"Every single chapter of Maja's work brings insights which touch us all. The more we follow her insights the closer we move to the universal truth and nature."

PROF. DR. TADEJA JERE JAKULIN, Slovenia

———

"The book guides you with grace and discipline towards your true objectives. Really worth the experience."

MARIA ANSELMI, Group Director Bisnode AB, Switzerland

Stop chasing weekends

MORE REVIEWS AT:
www.stopchasingweekends.com

FOREWORD

"Mum, why did you write this book?" my 7-year-old daughter Luna asked me one day. Hmm, what a good question! I wrote it because I felt I should. Because I wanted to share my story to help women who constantly struggle with balancing work-home-family and, in doing so, often forget about their own needs – like I used to do. Because I know that even small changes can lead to a happier and more meaningful life.

This book reveals all the colours of my life – but actually it could be the life of any other woman. I'd especially like to thank Dr Tadeja Jere Jakulin, a wonderful person, a teacher and practitioner of the Colour Mirrors system. She helped me unleash my full potential and gave a meaning to my path, for which I'm forever grateful.

Here is what she has to say about this book:

Every little girl has a dream; to be either a princess or a hero. But what if that little girl suddenly became both? A princess and a hero! Maja's journey through life, as she describes in her book, started just like the journey of many little girls; with being diligent, working hard and being hard – on herself and consequently on life. She subconsciously lived in fear. Yet life offered her many opportunities to face up to her fears and overcome them.

Today, Maja no longer spends her days dreaming her life away; her dreams come true and now she wants to share the secret of how to make dreams become a reality. She knows exactly what she wants and goes for it. Best of all, she wants to share the wisdom she's gained through facing challenges in her life. The fears have gone and only challenges and heroic thoughts remain. This little princess has become the hero of her life; she knows when to say goodbye to old patterns, consciousness, and knows when to make a shift.

Her book expresses the natural path of human life, the flow that requires listening to your inner self, appreciation of experiences, learning and staying focused. These days people, primarily women, spread their energy around thinly, and let their thoughts rule their day, creating a lack of focus and time. Is it really so difficult to discover our mission and retain it as the common thread running through our life? Yes, difficult – but not impossible.

Maja shows how making our own rules and sticking to them accompanied by good self-esteem guides you toward fulfilling your mission; a mission filled with friends, soulmates, and gratefulness. Gratefulness is important – it beats your ego and wakens your creativity.

Every single chapter of Maja's work brings insights which touch us all. The more we follow her insights the closer we move to the universal truth and nature. She guides us towards happiness and success; the more you love your mission that brings you constant changes, the more successful you are, and the clearer you see the value of your life.

Follow the wisdom of her book and you'll find this wisdom within you.

Prof. Dr. Tadeja Jere Jakulin

ONE DAY YOU WILL WAKE UP AND
THERE WON'T BE ANY TIME LEFT
TO DO THE THINGS
YOU'VE ALWAYS WANTED.

DO IT NOW.

— PAULO COELHO —

1. PREFACE

It was the end of yet another ordinary day, but little did I know that was all about to change; driving home from work, we were involved in a head-on collision – a woman driving on our side of the road went straight into us. The car was totally smashed but, to our amazement we were both fine, we managed to survive without even a scratch.

———

Immediately after the incident I felt fine, I mean I wasn't panicking – it seemed as if I would simply get over it. But, after a few hours, once the adrenalin had worn off, I started reliving the whole experience; I started shaking uncontrollably as it suddenly hit me – it's a sign, a warning: Life is too short to wait for another chance, to postpone things I've always wanted to do, to see, to achieve – the time is NOW!

Later that evening, I sat down at my laptop and started writing. I had wanted to do that for quite some time, but just never seemed to find the time. Most of my time was taken up with work and my clients – I even put it before my children. So wrong.

It's amazing how priorities can change overnight. If it hadn't been for the woman driving into us, I'd still be living my life today as I was then – thinking there'd always be a tomorrow. That's why today, I'm extremely thankful for that day, which literally woke me up and helped make my dream, the one you're holding in your hands, come true.

This a true story about how I learned to balance my work with my personal life and started living again. It wasn't always easy: there were ups and downs along the way, from which I discovered a lot, especially about myself, so that today I can live my life the way I have always wanted.

I hope my story will encourage you to open your heart and be sincere about who you are, what you really want from your life and what's holding you back from achieving it.

At the end of each chapter, you'll find key takeaways and questions for reflection. They will help you find your own way to manifest your dreams and desires and get the life you've always wanted.

I'm delighted to present you with four women who have touched me in a special way and inspired me to step onto my new life path. Publishing their stories is my way of saying 'thank you'. Let them inspire you to start creating the changes you want to see in your life and in the world around you.

Life is a gift – don't waste it. It doesn't matter who you are, how old you are, where you live, or what you do for a living. All that matters is that you START, right from where you are. So take your first step towards a new, more balanced and happier life filled with everything you've always dreamed of! Enjoy your journey!

THIS BOOK IS FOR YOU BECAUSE ...

... IT IS JUST AS MUCH YOUR STORY AS IT IS MINE:

- to show you that you're not alone,
- to help you discover your strengths,
- to help you nurture your passions and build your life around them,
- to help you get rid of your limiting beliefs,
- to help you find answers to those questions, preventing you moving forward,
- to help you find your inner peace, and
- TO CREATE THE LIFE YOU DESERVE!

It's YOUR life, it's YOUR time, it's YOUR game – so stop chasing weekends, make EVERY DAY count!

A DREAM
IS A WISH YOUR
HEART
MAKES.

— WALT DISNEY —

2. A GIRL WITH A DREAM

Remember when you were a little girl? When everything seemed possible? When you had no limits, there were no voices inside your head saying you won't make it, telling you to stop? No fears or doubts whatsoever? When every new experience was an adventure you could hardly wait to start?

Even after all these years, the image of that little girl is so vivid; I was so brave, fearless and ready for new adventures. I had a pretty good idea of what I wanted to become and how I wanted my life to be.

On one of my visits to my mom's house, I started digging through some drawers in my old room. Like most doting mothers, she keeps an archive of my childhood – old photos, my favorite toys, school notebooks, and stuff I've forgotten about long ago.

All kinds of fond memories came flooding back whilst going through my stuff; an old address book with all my friends' contacts (ha, who needs this these days with Facebook?), ageing photos from high school trips, old postcards and letters, poems from a secret admirer....

However, my attention was drawn to a piece of paper titled "How do I see myself in 20 years?" To my surprise, I realized I was holding the very first essay I'd written in high school.

Like most teenagers, high school was a big milestone for me; a big city, new people, changing my lifestyle and the added novelty of travelling to another city every day. The city kids saw us commuters (country kids) as outsiders who'd just arrived from the Stone Age. I can still hear my snobby classmates asking: "Do you even have a store in your town? Do you have telephones?" The reality was that my town was just 53 kilometers from the capital where my school was – I mean, Slovenia is a small place.

Nevertheless, I remember how angry I'd get, and how I didn't like the city kids, but it was their taunting and my stubbornness that motivated my teenage self to become one of the top students in class. I wanted to show them that where you're from doesn't define who you are, even if I was from a small town.

With so many memories of my 15-year-old self running through my mind, I started reading. I couldn't believe it; word after word, paragraph after paragraph I painted a picture of my dream world with unlimited possibilities for the future there – describing a perfect life, full of hopes and dreams.

I had dreams of finishing university, learning foreign languages, so I could travel the world, meet new people and explore different cultures. I had a dream of having my own company, so I could do whatever I wanted whenever I wanted. This last one was almost certainly a reaction to watching my journalist father, working late nights, smoking like a chimney whilst furiously typing on his old typewriter to meet his deadline.

I had a dream about a happy family, a loving husband, cute children and a nice house. And, finally, I had a dream about living in London.

The vision was so clear, so precisely written, that it gave me goose bumps. I was quite surprised that even back then, 30 years ago, I knew exactly what I wanted. Now I know that by writing it down I had unintentionally created my very own reality about what was about to happen.

Then a question popped into my head: what happened to that girl? So fun, so romantic, so optimistic, and full of life? Where did that beautiful young woman who thought she could have it all go?

I realized I'd lost her somewhere along the way and I started feeling sorry for her and all her dreams left behind, buried, and forgotten. The outside world had intervened, and she'd been swept away by what others wanted and expected from her. Now, I wanted to bring that girl back!

A CHALLENGE FOR YOU:

WHAT DID YOU DREAM ABOUT WHEN YOU WERE A LITTLE GIRL? WHAT ARE YOU DREAMING ABOUT NOW?

1. Describe your ideal life in as much detail as possible. Write as if it's already happened, using "I have", "I am" and not "I want to…"
2. Read it through. If anything is missing, edit and rewrite it until you've got the ideal picture of your life.
3. Now close your eyes and visualize yourself living the life you've just written about. Vivid pictures of yourself in situations you've just described, with the people you mention, at the job

you want, at the places you want to go to, doing the things you dream of.

4. Find a box to put this paper in. Hide it in a secret place, but not so secret that you won't find it again as you'll need to add more things to it.

CONGRATULATIONS, STEP 1 COMPLETE!

WINNERS
ARE DREAMERS WHO
NEVER GIVE UP.

— NELSON MANDELA —

3. WORK HARD, PLAY HARD

Finally, my dream destination: London! I was holding an airline ticket in my hand and screaming like a kid just given her favorite toy. I had been dreaming of London ever since I was a teenager. In my eyes, this city represented everything my childhood dream stood for: meeting people from all over the world and all walks of life, the diversity of living with modern skyscrapers on one side and cozy neighborhoods on the other, limitless chances for expressing individuality, numerous opportunities to find a great job and, last but not least, freedom. Not that I didn't have all of that, but for me London was THE thing.

During my twenties, I worked in a corporate environment. When I started in 1992, Studio Moderna was a small company, with one office, two desks, two phones, two students, each with a notebook into which we carefully put down every customer's name and address. We were selling a single product, a back pain relief device via direct response channels. At that time, I had no idea this product would forever seal my fate.

Over the years, the firm added new products to its product portfolio and expanded its operations to new European markets. In a few years, it grew into a direct marketing network across Europe with a few thousand employees. And as the firm grew, so did I. While working, I took time to write my diploma paper and successfully graduated from the Faculty of Economics.

The firm was also very generous when it comes to investing in the knowledge and education of its employees. We were sent abroad, mostly to the USA where we learned from the world's best direct marketing experts. Something most people can only dream about OR perhaps read about in those people's books; a priceless experience for a young and ambitious woman in her mid-twenties.

I had a dream job many people would die for. I was traveling a lot, mostly abroad – with destinations including New York, San Francisco, Los Angeles, Chicago, Toronto, Monte Carlo, Venice, even to Bangkok, Thailand and Cancun, Mexico to name just a few, sleeping in the best hotels, dining at top restaurants, meeting people from all over the world. Living the life I'd always wanted.

If I wasn't at a business conference or on a business trip to meet suppliers, then I was visiting one of our European offices, where I'd monitor the realization of marketing plans and consult local teams on how to improve the performance of their marketing activities. There were months when I spent more days traveling than at home, in Slovenia. I'd sometimes wake up in the morning, and need a minute just to remember where I actually was.

When I wasn't traveling, I was in the office, working. I could say I was at work most of the time. Not that anybody told me to, there was just so much going on. I was so eager to learn and took every opportunity to acquire new experiences: the feeling was addictive. On top of my regular work, I spent many evenings, even nights at the studio, supervising adaptations of TV commercials. I was lucky enough to be surrounded by a great team of people, with whom I always had fun. I simply enjoyed it, my work was like a drug and it became my way of life.

My old friends slowly lost patience and interest in inviting me to join them for after-work drinks, going to the movies or just hanging out as I was always too busy or something important just came up. Last-minute cancellations became my signature move that I definitely wasn't proud of. So my work colleagues also became the people I hung out with after work and on weekends.

At the end of 1998, I started working on my dream project: to open an office in London. Everyone knew London had been my dream city since I was a teenager. I had saved pocket money throughout high school so I could take an English summer course at the London Business School the year I left high school. Besides that, a fortune teller had once told me that I would live in a big city beginning with "L". Of course, I was sure it could mean nothing but London.

I already saw myself walking beside the Thames and listening to Big Ben while having a lunch break ... but it was not to be.

I was sitting at Warsaw airport with the company owner, Sandi Češko, after a few days' visit to our Polish offices, waiting for the fog to clear so our flight could take off. He suddenly turned to me and said: "Maja, you'll have to come here again soon and stay a bit longer." Of course, I said, no problem. Frankly speaking, I thought it'd be for a week or so, but after a while I realized what he really meant. I was going to have to move to Warsaw as Poland was our most important market and the team in Warsaw needed on-site support. I was part of the solution.

The decision was made and I had 14 days to pack my bags, organize everything, and move to Warsaw. I was still so enthusiastic about London that I thought of Warsaw as just an intermediary challenge. When Sandi heard about it, he smiled at me and, familiar with the 'L city' story from the fortuneteller, he said: "La Warsaw is just as good if not even better." It became an office joke and soon I was on my way to Warsaw.

The company rented me a nice flat at 132 Ostrobramska street, just ten minutes' drive from the office. During the week, I'd work till evening, come home late, do some more work, have a glass of wine or two and a cigarette before going to bed. Weekends were for hanging around Warsaw with friends or by myself, or just doing nothing in my little lonely world.

I learned to speak Polish in a few months so I could easily argue with taxi drivers who would regularly try to rip me off by driving me around and around the city. As sales figures started to rise and business improved, I realized that a year and a half had gone by since I had gone on my little 'trip' to Warsaw. During my time in Warsaw, I made a lot of good friends, had a good life, while still running the same lifestyle: working round the clock.

It wasn't until I got a flattering job offer from a reputable Polish company that I really started to assess my lifestyle choice. After meeting the CEO, I later sat down in my flat and started writing out some pros and cons; should I stay where I am? Should I take the job? That would mean staying in Warsaw. Am I ready to spend a few more years here? What do I really want?

There were many questions and, to my surprise, many remained unanswered. But while trying to find some answers it suddenly hit me: next year, I'll be 30 years old! Half of my life has already gone by! What the hell am I doing? I need to get a life! I don't want to stay here. I want to go back to Slovenia!

Having taken stock, I realized that besides my amazingly glamorous lifestyle, which I really enjoyed, the years had quickly passed me by and I was nearly 30. Outside of work I had no life, and the fact remained that I was lonely. I was stuck in a rut that was preventing me from getting to what I was longing for: to settle down, find the love of my life, and have a family and children. I was in desperate need for change.

I discussed this with Sandi who wasn't too happy to hear about my wish to return home, but we eventually managed to come to an agreement. I packed my bags and said 'Goodbye' to Warsaw and 'Hello' to Slovenia!

KEY TAKEAWAYS

- Don't let planning get in the way of going with the flow; the latter is sometimes the better option.
- Take every opportunity to learn, explore the world and meet new people – a priceless experience.
- Learn from every situation and every person you meet. Funny how sometimes someone you don't expect anything from can teach you the best lesson.
- No matter how good or bad life is, stay true to yourself and stay focused on what you really want.

TWENTY YEARS FROM NOW, YOU WILL BE MORE
DISAPPOINTED BY THE THINGS THAT YOU DIDN'T
DO THAN BY THE ONES YOU DID DO.
SO THROW OFF THE BOWLINES.
SAIL AWAY FROM THE SAFE HARBOR.
CATCH THE TRADE WINDS IN YOUR SAILS.
EXPLORE. DREAM. DISCOVER.

— MARK TWAIN —

4. TIME TO SAY GOODBYE

Sometimes you live your life and don't even realize that you're stuck in everyday routines, tight deadlines and suffocating relationships. Not until something (usually unexpected) happens. But sometimes just a simple question is enough to change the way you look at things.

It was October 2000 when I returned to Slovenia. It felt as if I had never left, everything felt the same. I had no difficulties adjusting to my old everyday routine. The only problem was that while I was gone my apartment had been rented out, so I had to stay with my parents until I found a new place to stay. As you can imagine, after having lived on my own for almost a decade, this was a nightmare; I just wasn't used to having anyone around me anymore. The mornings were tough – I was used to having my morning coffee in silence and now I had the hustle and bustle of the family home to contend with.

I fell straight back into the nine to five, most days I was at the office even longer. My social life was non-existent as lots of my so-called friends had forgotten I existed the minute I moved to Poland and was no longer holding huge media budgets in my hands (oh yes, I realized that for some people you're only as important as your annual budget). I was miserable, bitter and tired of my pace of life, which I no longer enjoyed.

Finally, I found a flat in Ljubljana and moved out of my parents' house.

Winter was well underway in the Slovenian capital and New Year's Eve was just around the corner. As usual for the 'biggest night of the year', I had no plans. My cousin Mateja called me and suggested we go celebrate on the streets of Ljubljana. I was more than surprised because she and her long-term boyfriend almost never went out. So the prospect of going to an outdoor event with a mass of people I didn't know on a cold winter's night with my loved-up cousin sounded good enough for me – so I joined them. I was looking forward to spending time with them, but had no expectations about the party aspect whatsoever. I didn't think for one second that this would be THE turning point of my life.

If someone predicted you were going to meet the man of your dreams, the love of your life on a New Year's eve, on the street, amid a crowd of 30,000 people, would you believe them? Probably not, too cliché – but this is exactly what happened!

Midnight had already struck and I was dancing with my friends in one of Ljubljana's town squares to live music. As I was doing my 'thang' to the music, I accidentally grabbed someone's arm. He was tall, had long blond hair and was the most handsome man I'd ever seen. He was wearing sexy red jeans and a brown leather jacket. I'll never forget the moment our eyes met. He stopped and wished me "Happy New Year", but our conversation didn't stop there, saying "Happy lifetime" would've been more appropriate. From the very first moment we met, I felt like I had known him forever. We talked like old friends for hours – it was just natural and the time was flowing. We couldn't get enough of each other; our first date followed a week later, and a month later Aco moved in with me. And stayed forever!

I was in heaven. I had never imagined how strongly love could strike. Not me; I'm too strong, too rational. Or was I?

All of a sudden, my life took on another meaning. I was looking forward to every morning, I couldn't wait to come back home to be with him. I still traveled a lot, but it just wasn't fun anymore. I missed him too much if he wasn't around.

Meanwhile, the company was growing fast. Consultants from abroad were often popping in and out of our offices, talking to management, interviewing employees and going back to management to tell them the same things we had told them before, but they wouldn't listen.

I was one of five regional directors at the time and during an interview with a consultant, he threw the all too common question at me: "Where do you see yourself in five years?" Hmmm, I wasn't ready for that question. I was kind of satisfied with my life at that moment: I had a dream job; the salary was great, bonuses as well. I was in a relationship with a man I loved – life was quite good. Although the truth was that most of my life was still built around the company as my work defined the pace of my life.

The question triggered something inside of me. I took a few moments to answer, then I heard my voice saying: "Five years from now, I see myself with my own consulting firm."

I guess the consultant was as startled as I was. He said "No, no, I mean within THIS company." But it was already too late: the seed was planted and there was no way back.

I started dreaming of what it would be like to have my own company. The freedom to do what I knew best, what I really loved, without having to wait for approval, make compromises on things I didn't want to make compromises on, and less traveling so I could spend more time with the man I love.

The thought of having my own company and starting from scratch was exciting, yet scary. I was aware that, even though I had a lot of professional knowledge and vast international experience, world's best in class teachers, great performance results for my current company, nobody in Slovenia (except for a few media directors) really knew me outside the company.

Nevertheless, that didn't scare me. The more I thought about it, the more critical (or maybe objective?) I became in the way I saw my current job and the company's everyday operations.

A year later, I finally made the decision: I went to the CEO and handed in my resignation. He didn't take me seriously at first. But after talking to me, he realized my mind was made up.

A few meetings on the topic followed: at first, he tried to convince me how 'dangerous' it was to start from scratch in a market where nobody knew me. Damn, that was exactly what I didn't want to hear. The next meeting was about conditions to stay – I made it perfectly clear that I wasn't there to negotiate and that I had made my mind up. I told him I wanted to start my own consulting business to share my know-how and help companies become more effective in marketing. I saw a great opportunity in the outside world, ruled by traditional advertising agencies that knew nothing about direct response accountability. The third meeting went in the complete opposite direction: he asked me to tell him which resources I needed to do what I planned, but within his firm.

As tempting as it might've sounded (wow, starting a business with a dream budget and dream conditions), I said no. The scent of freedom was too sweet (although I must admit now that some pocket money would've come in handy in the first two years).

Whilst all of these changes were going on in my life, I suffered a great unexpected loss – my father passed away. Only a day before his death, he had driven 150 kilometers just to see me, like he had anticipated what was going to happen and wanted to say goodbye. And the next day he was gone. It shook me and made me think. It made me look at my own life and how impermanent we all are. I became aware that we're all just trespassing here and, no matter how long we live, we just don't get another chance.

The loss of my father made me even more determined in my decision to push boundaries and step into a new, unknown direction – something he was constantly doing during his life. Unfortunately, only when he was gone did I realize how alike we both were and how much I could've learned from him. If only we had been given more time – but it was too late.

Three months later, I said goodbye to Studio Moderna and started my new business endeavor.

A CHALLENGE FOR YOU:

WHAT OR WHOM DO YOU NEED TO LET GO OF FROM YOUR LIFE?

- Where do you see yourself in five years?
- Are there doors you need to close because you feel they no longer lead anywhere? Is there someone you no longer feel comfortable around?
- What part of your life do you WANT to change?
- Does that decision/step take you closer/further from what you want?

EVERY RISK IS WORTH TAKING AS LONG AS IT'S FOR A GOOD CAUSE, AND CONTRIBUTES TO A GOOD LIFE.

— RICHARD BRANSON —

5. OVERCOMING **FEAR** OF THE UNKNOWN

When I quit my job, I was met with disbelief from my friends, co-workers and colleagues – everybody told me I was crazy. You just don't quit a perfect job with a great salary, bonuses, and company car. Frankly, I was scared. For the first time in my life, I was completely on my own. Crazy enough to believe that just by showing up in the business arena and offering services that no other marketing agency on the market offered, my business would be an overnight success. As it turned out, it wasn't that easy.

My last day at work was December 31st, 2001. In the last few months before I left, I put together a white paper with clear and precise instructions for the team and finished all my outstanding projects. On the last day, I cleaned my desk, returned the office and car keys, while thanking and saying goodbye to my colleagues. We had a few farewell drinks at a nearby bar, and then I left.

I received many letters of support, including one from the Richard Rosen, one of the top direct marketing experts in the USA and my greatest role model, who wrote: "Go for it … from the moment I met you, I knew you'd be gone if the firm didn't keep you educated and stimulated with great marketing wisdom. If I can be of any assistance, I'd love to help, seriously, would enjoy working with you. I always thought you might come here and work for us for a year …" It was a huge inspiration because I really valued and respected him and his opinion.

So here I was, having moved from the top position of international marketing director for 11 countries of a worldwide highly reputable company to a startup, a one-man band nobody has ever heard of. Within a few months I had put my business plan together, registered a company and put up a new website.

Deciding on a company name took quite some time: I wanted it to communicate what the company was all about, what our mission was: connecting companies with customers, building valuable relationships between them. After a few brainstorming sessions with Aco, we came down to a list of about 50 names, dealing with synonyms for connections, connecting, uniting… we eventually picked "Spago", an Italian word meaning rope while, at the same time, it uses the first letters of both our surnames, Aco's and mine. Spago was officially born on January 11th, 2002.

At that time, I had no idea how the company would get clients. As the company was literally an unknown entity in the market, Aco decided to keep his job at the bank just to be on the safe side, so at least we'd have one steady income.

We moved from Ljubljana to his parents' house near the coast to cut our living costs. It was a huge change for me: while dreaming about London, I had moved from Warsaw (population of some 2 million) back to Ljubljana (population of some 300,000) only to land up in a small village, 20 minutes from the seaside, with 24 houses, surrounded by beautiful nature, in the middle of nowhere, without any shop or bar, nothing; a place where you wake up with birds singing instead of the sound of cars honking. It was quite a challenge for me to switch from living on my own, which I had been doing the last ten years, to being back under someone else's roof. Luckily, we had our own apartment on the first floor with a separate entrance, so I got used to the new situation pretty fast.

At the beginning I worked from home, actually from my living room, where I had a desk with a computer and a phone. That was enough. At first, I focused solely on consulting and showing our clients new opportunities for growth by concentrating more on building valuable relationships with their customers, and then left it up to them to make it happen. Luckily, I learned from the first project that it wouldn't work out that way – no matter how good the idea was, poor execution could easily kill it. So I started building a team that would help bring my ideas to life.

Livija Dolanc, the first CEO of Studio Moderna and Sandi's wife, once told me that no matter how good you are or how much you know, if nobody knows you exist, it won't do you any good. So I started writing 'how to' articles about what I knew best: direct marketing and direct sales and published them on the Spago website.

I joined various trade organizations and started attending networking events. I monitored the website's traffic and realized that, by looking at the e-newsletter subscriber list, I could get a pretty good idea of what companies were looking for and thereby define which company to contact next. And that was the direction I took.

Back in 2002, most marketers and advertising agencies looked down on direct response marketing as it was mistakenly interpreted as TV shopping and thus not fancy enough. Also, clients were not used to the questions we were asking like what response rates were, how many leads converted to buyers, what was cost per order etc. Wrong questions! They were still the times when advertisers didn't know which 50% of the budget brought the results. And most of them didn't really care. However, some clients recognized the advantages of the approach we had adopted as it provided the accountability that was demanded by top management.

In the first year, we signed Slovenia's biggest pharmaceutical company and soon after a national mobile operator. Three years later, I was earning more than my previous salary. Aco joined the team and took over some accounts. We hired more people to support Spago's growth. Things only kept on going skyward.

As word got around, top Slovenian companies from all industries were knocking on our door, usually wanting us to handle projects or brands that were in trouble. Our results proved we could walk the talk; as we helped our clients build valuable relationships with their customers, they helped build our business by recommending us to their partners. Our business was mostly built on references and referrals.

Just imagine a client that every (and I mean EVERY) marketing agency would die for, approaching us and literally saying: "We want you, we know you're the best with direct communications." The next thing you know, you have a signed contract on the table. YES!!!

There were two things we never compromised on: respect for clients and responsibility for our work and results. On two occasions we even terminated a contract with a client due to its unethical business practices – we didn't want to have anything to do with that.

However, there were also times when I wasn't sure anymore whether it was ok to do the right thing; especially after we were awarded a communication efficiency award, one of the most prestigious awards in the industry – the sound of whistles from our competitors when our name was called out still echoes in my ears. I knew we had been a pain in the neck to the big advertising agencies, but it was only after this event that I realized why and to what extent.

They were used to playing with big budgets; their way of doing business never provided the client with the exact answer about where the money was worth spending. And here we were, a small agency, proving how effectively every penny had been spent, testing every step, trying new approaches and not wasting any client's money. Oh yes, they didn't like us at all.

But, as times changed and advertising lost its power, even the big guys wanted to be like us. One of the largest advertising agencies approached us and offered us a partnership – and because we said no, we had to give up some of our best clients – yes, that's what happens when you play against the big guys who have all the power and limitless measures. However, we survived.

In a little over a decade, we grew and developed Spago from a home-based business to an enterprise providing strategic customer relationship marketing solutions. I was elected Head of Direct Marketing and Sales Section within the Slovenian Marketing Association, a huge acknowledgement for all the years of hard work and projects for the most prominent companies from all industries.

I started to share my experience at major marketing events, as a guest professor at Gea College and to train employees at workshops in many reputable companies. It's great to see individuals growing personally, improving their performance and thereby improving the business results of the organizations they work for.

Despite how scared I was at the prospect of starting up on my own, I never regretted my decision. I worked even harder, but the harder the work, the more enjoyment I seemed to find in it. Above all, the freedom to do what I loved and the feedback I got from clients was just too sweet to trade for anything. It was the start of a beautiful new era. Today, as I look back, I'm grateful for each and every moment.

A CHALLENGE FOR YOU:

WHAT WOULD YOU DO IF YOU WEREN'T AFRAID?

1. Write a list of things you've always wanted to do, but were afraid to try for various reasons.
2. Now prioritize what's on the list: what means the most to you?
3. Take your number one priority. Which steps do you have to take to reach that goal? Write them down.
4. After writing down the steps, ask yourself what you need to do to make each of those steps happen?
5. How can you get what you need? Where can you get it? Who can help you with it? Or is it just you who needs to get your head in the game?
6. Next to each step, write the date. Mark the day and task in your calendar – this is the day when you'll actually take a step towards fulfilling your dream.
7. Just do it. Be brave. Everything you want is on the other side of fear.

SOMETIMES WHAT
YOU'RE LOOKING FOR
COMES WHEN YOU'RE
NOT LOOKING AT ALL.

6. HOW TO DEAL WITH SITUATIONS YOU **CAN'T PLAN**

To the outside world we had a dream life many people would die for. Over the years, our relationship had become even stronger. Business was good and prosperous; we were making a nice, comfortable living. However, only a few people knew that, away from all eyes and ears, we had been struggling hard for the last eight years. It was a struggle that seemed to have no happy ending.

———

The doctor looked straight into my eyes and said with a poker face: "Let's face it, you're too old!" My world instantly collapsed before me. For the first time ever, I felt completely helpless.

For eight years we had been struggling to get pregnant. If you're someone who plans everything in life very carefully and also achieves everything according to plan, it's really hard to understand there's something in your life you can't plan.

We had tried various fertility treatments, natural, traditional medicine, and homeopathic remedies but nothing seemed to work. We decided to try the last possible option, in-vitro fertilization (IVF); eggs from my ovaries were removed and then fertilized with sperm in a laboratory. If the procedure was successful and the egg was fertilized, the embryo would be returned to my uterus. It's not as painful as it is stressful. Two to three weeks before the procedure, I had to undergo hormone treatments which meant that every morning I had to give myself a hormone shot.

The effects were not very pleasant: my stomach looked like I was 3 months pregnant, I was anxious and often on the verge of tears. At the time of ovulation the doctor monitored the size of the eggs on a daily basis. For us, that meant waking up at 4.30 am, driving an hour to the clinic, joining other women quietly sitting in the waiting room and waiting for my name to be called. We were all going through the same; doing everything to make our greatest wish come true, to become a mom.

Our whole life was focused on getting pregnant. After each unsuccessful procedure, the disappointment was bigger and harder to bear. It occupied our mind, our life – we were both under great stress. Due to the constant hormone treatments, I gained a lot of weight, but I didn't really care how I looked. I didn't buy myself any new clothes because in my mind I was 'getting pregnant' all the time. I was a nervous wreck. I found escape in work, piled up more projects and put myself under more stress. It was a vicious cycle I didn't know how to escape from.

We had eight IVF procedures, at two different fertility clinics with top experts. On the way, we lost our hope and even gave up for a while. But it came back. After the last, eighth unsuccessful IVF, we decided to go with the flow: no more appointments with doctors, no more hormones.

The whole experience was a huge test for our partnership. At times, I wasn't sure if we were going to make it. We discussed adoption and other options, but decided that if we were not going to have our own children, we might as well live without them. After all, there are other beautiful aspects of life and so we agreed we'd better start enjoying it. We started planning our summer vacations and booked a trip to the USA later in the fall.

In the meantime, we started working on a new project. It was actually a cruise for our client's partner. I knew the company, but didn't know the person responsible as our client was in contact with the partner.

At the first official project meeting, we were all sitting in the meeting room and waiting for their marketing director to arrive. The door opened and I just couldn't believe my eyes. Standing in front of us was a good friend, a man I had held a very good business relationship with in my previous job as we had been sponsors of the organization he was an active member of.

He was as astonished and surprised to see me as I was to see him. We hugged in front of everyone, much to the bewilderment of those around us. We had a lot of catching up to do as we hadn't seen each other in ten years. There were plenty of opportunities as we spent quite some time together in the following months.

But my friend Andrej already had another business idea he wanted to discuss with Aco and myself. We met for dinner and, after hearing what it was all about, agreed to take part in the project. He suggested that prior to taking the first steps, he'd take us to a biotherapist to check and see whether or not we're compatible on an energetic level.

It was August 15th, 2008. Enver, the biotherapist, was sitting behind a desk in his little corner office. The minute he held my hand and laid his eyes on Aco and myself, he said he wanted to talk with us in private. When we were alone in the room, he started talking to us like he had known us forever – to my surprise, he was reading us like an open book. I had never seen or experienced anything like that in my life before.

He brought up our unfulfilled wish to have a child. He told us not to lose hope and that everything would work out: if only we followed his instructions and his therapy, I'd be pregnant by Christmas. Well, I hated this man at that moment; bringing back hopes that had just been buried, although deep inside they were still so much alive. At the same time, what he was saying was against everything I believed: to me, traditional medicine was the one and only. I trusted people in white coats and believed their words.

After listening to what he had to say, we decided we'd give it a try. We really had nothing to lose. So we started with biotherapies, visiting him three times a month, not missing a single appointment and carefully sticking to all his instructions.

The fall came and our trip to the United States of America to the annual conference of the Direct Marketing Association. The world's largest event for direct marketing professionals that attracted around 14,000 people was the biggest event I'd ever been to. That year it took place in Las Vegas. Seven days packed with workshops and classes, from morning until evening. Important fuel for our business ideas but, on the other hand, a crazy place we didn't like much.

After the conference we took a few extra days off and spent them in Los Angeles. Although I'd been there a few times before, it was so much more enjoyable with Aco. We had a great time: we went sightseeing, visited Beverly Hills, Bel Air, took photos with the famous Hollywood sign, shopped on Rodeo Drive, walked around Hollywood and searched for our favorite actors' names on the famous Walk of Fame. The day we spent at Venice Beach was my favorite. We'd forgotten about our real life and problems back home.

Just a few days after returning home, we were packing our bags again for the cruise. I must admit that even though I had traveled a lot in my life, this cruise was one of my greatest traveling experiences. Every day we woke up in another city, even another country, got off the ship to see where we'd landed, and did some sightseeing and enjoyed local food. The evenings were spent on the ship, in the theater or one of the numerous cocktail bars, until we all gathered on the top deck in the club where we danced until morning, when the cycle began again. We had a great time.

The cruise was a great success: the client was happy and the whole team had a wonderful time. The project even served as a best practice in the travel industry as it was the first time a company had organized an event in the form of a seven-day cruise for its customers.

When we got back from this trip, I was a little tired. I thought it was because I wasn't used to so much partying. At the same time, I was dragged quickly into my heavy daily routine, too much of everything, too much work, and too much stress. Nothing unusual. But then my period was late. It had happened before, but we had been disappointed so many times over negative pregnancy test results that I didn't even tell Aco.

But after two weeks and still no period I secretly bought a pregnancy test. That night I waited for Aco to fall asleep. I quietly smuggled it into the bathroom, took the test and ... there it was, the surprise of a lifetime. It was POSITIVE!!! I couldn't believe my eyes as I gazed at the two lines in the small window. I was finally pregnant!

Nine months later, I gave birth to a wonderful little girl Luna, which means 'the Moon' in Slovenian, who became the sunshine of my life from the moment she was born. I simply couldn't have wished for more. I'll be grateful to Andrej and Enver for the rest of my life.

KEY TAKEAWAYS:

- Every person crosses your path for a reason. While it might not be obvious at first, sooner or later everything will become clear.
- Sometimes you have to let go and go with the flow.
- Everything will be all right. If it's not all right, it's still not the end.

YOU CAN PLAN
THE PERFECT PICNIC
BUT YOU CAN'T
PREDICT THE WEATHER.

— ANDRÉ LAUREN BENJAMIN —

7. EVERYTHING HAPPENS FOR A REASON

I thought I had it all planned out. My little girl was in kindergarten and growing. I was pregnant with my second baby. Business was stable so we could afford to employ a new person as I was slowly getting ready to fully devote my time to the new little being about to come into this world. I had no idea everything would change overnight.

———

When I had my first baby, Luna, I really took time off from work and devoted all my attention to her. My daily routine consisted of breastfeeding, changing diapers, going for walks, playing with her, breastfeeding again and so on and so on. I didn't miss the adrenaline at work, I didn't miss clients and, honestly, I didn't think about them. I was only occupied with my precious little girl.

After a year, she went to kindergarten and I went back to work. Boy was it hard! The scope of work had increased a lot; there were ever more clients and more projects. Very soon I was back to my normal working rhythm from morning till evening, and at the same time feeling guilty for not spending more time with my little girl.

When Luna was one and a half years old, I started feeling sick again. We'd just returned from a spring cruise across the Mediterranean when I took a pregnancy test. It was positive again! When I looked back, I remembered there were some clues already on the cruise: I was so tired when we embarked in Barcelona, after the trip to Rome I was lying half dead in bed – to be honest, most evenings on the ship I fell asleep even before my baby girl. Not that we planned it – actually after having had so many difficulties getting pregnant with Luna, we didn't even dare dream of having another baby. But here it was and we were blessed!

Before I was due with my second baby, I had carefully planned everything: informed our clients that I'd be gone for a while, delegated my projects and tasks to my colleagues, negotiated and signed annual deals so the company would have a stable income. Yes, everything – exactly like any proper control freak would do.

It was mid-December, a month before my due date, when one of our colleagues stood up and proclaimed: "that's it, I quit". WHAT? What happened? Come on, you can't just quit! Apparently, the client had been giving her a hard time for a while and she had simply had enough. We tried to calm her down, suggested taking a few days off to rethink the whole situation and come back. But her mind was already made up. She left and never returned.

Come on, NOT a month before my due date!!! A new employee was coming in February, but I knew I couldn't leave Aco on his own to drown in projects! One thing I've learned over the years is that when someone's made their mind up, don't try to stop them. It soon became obvious that our colleague just needed an excuse, as she had made her decision long before.

As though the situation wasn't bad enough already, a week later I started getting cramps and on a wonderful Christmas morning I delivered Luka, a cute baby boy. Wow, we were all so happy that for a while I forgot about the situation at work.

However, after the New Year's holidays were over, it soon became clear the year was not going to be a party. We just couldn't wait for the new employee to start working – we welcomed her with our hands wide open. Yes, everything would be all right now, I could go back to breast feeding, changing diapers, and the other pleasantries of being the mother of a newborn.

However, it was just the beginning of a nightmare. In mid-February we received an invitation from the same client that had made our employee resign, to participate in an agency pitch for the region. For those who aren't from the marketing world: an agency pitch is an invitation by a client to prepare a proposal or solution to promote a product or a service or solve a particular business problem the client is facing. Usually two or more agencies are invited. The client then chooses one of them to sign the contract with. It would've been a great opportunity, if it wasn't in OUR specialty field, for the very same job and client we'd negotiated an annual contract for just two months before!

We had no idea what was going on. After chatting with the person responsible, who was also our contact person at the client, she ensured me it was just a matter of formality, that it was actually part of the reorganization process and a huge opportunity for us as we could actually expand and intensify our activities throughout the region.

So two months after having had a baby, I returned to work with Luka on my lap, breastfeeding every three hours and in between working on the proposal. For a month, the whole team worked really hard and came up with a great strategic solution. However, when it came to the presentation I felt something was off, it was obvious that someone had been misleading us from the outset. We found out later the deal was closed long before and that it was just a matter of a formality. I don't want to go into details, but it was a nasty game that was beyond our control. We were just too small a fish to swim with those sharks.

We'd lost an important account that represented a large portion of our revenue. We had a new employee with a huge salary who was supposed to be working on that project, sitting in the office. She was on the payroll, and money wasn't coming in.

The timing was not good for acquiring new clients. With a newborn, who had to be breastfed every few hours and a little girl in kindergarten, my mind was anywhere but in business. Yet we had to do something to bring in the lost revenue. We tried what had worked in the past, but whatever we tried, this time nothing seemed to bear fruit. It was the toughest year in the history of Spago.

One evening I was lying in bed, reading Paulo Coelho's novel Aleph. There was the sentence "if you want to get new ideas, you have to go out and meet new people". It touched me, stayed in my mind, and I just couldn't get rid of it.

So when a few weeks later we received an invitation from the Center for Entrepreneurship and Executive Development (CEED) to join a group of entrepreneurs who want to grow their businesses, Aco and I decided to grab the opportunity.

It turned out to be a great decision. For a few months we met every fortnight with a closed group of 12 entrepreneurs who faced the same challenges we did.

At the beginning, Aco and I were very hesitant to share too much about Spago, we were more listeners and participants in solving the others' problems. Then we realized what a great opportunity it was to have a brainstorming session and discuss some of our ideas and challenges with 12 people, from different backgrounds and industries. We opened up, swapped experiences more freely and shared opinions. It was a wonderful opportunity to get a second (and a third, and a fourth) opinion and also a chance to make ourselves better known within the community.

As a result, we started thinking differently. We saw great power and potential in networking. We met many great people, some of whom became our clients. Besides acquiring new business, we restructured our business to be less volatile to unexpected situations like the one that had caught us off guard.

If it wasn't for that unpleasant experience, if we hadn't lost that client, we probably wouldn't have had the need to search for new clients, nor the time to join CEED. If it wasn't for CEED, we wouldn't have met great new people and experienced wonderful new opportunities.

So at the end of the day, no matter how hard it was, I'm grateful for the experience as it enabled us to grow personally as well as professionally.

KEY TAKEAWAYS:

EVERYTHING HAPPENS FOR A REASON.

Sometimes when it happens, it hurts, you want to run away from it. But when you look back on it, you realize there was a reason it happened. You needed the experience to make you grow, to make you move forward, to make you stronger. Accept everything life has to offer. Look for the good in every situation and every person.

OUT OF YOUR
VULNERABILITIES
WILL COME
YOUR STRENGTH.

— SIGMUND FREUD —

8. THE SHIFT

I enjoyed the new dynamics of our life. Family life with kids brought a lot of exciting moments I'd have never dreamed of before. Although the fact there were no more peaceful moments of lying on the couch with a magazine or book when I wanted got to me from time to time. As did the fact I was no longer the master of my time.

For years it had only been me and my work. When I met Aco, it was him, me and work. Still, the focus was more on work than on 'us' and having time off. But now we had kids and it was really hard at first to shift perspective.

Maybe it was easier for me than Aco because when Luna was born, I spent a year without even popping into the office. I just didn't care. I was so much into the miracle of this new life and everything related to it that work was something I didn't even think about.

I enjoyed getting up in the morning, watching her open her eyes, having our time together while getting changed, nursing and playing with her. Whatever she did, I was ready with my camera and documented every single moment; dressed up in all her beautiful clothes, her first spoonful of solid food, her first step, her first sound... all my attention was given to her. She became the center of my universe. I was so obsessed with her I didn't let anyone hold her, let alone leave her with anyone for a few minutes. No, she was my precious little jewel. I adored her.

The closer we came to her first birthday, the more stressed out I became. I realized I'd have to let her go. And there she was, taking her first steps into kindergarten, making her first friends, crying her first tears for not being with me. But she survived, and so did I.

When Luka was born, it was a different story. Although we'd prepared Luna to be a big sister, she was very protective of her little brother, she demanded her space. I had the feeling she was asking for even more attention than before. I somehow expected she'd patiently wait for her turn while I was taking care of her little brother's basic needs, but that was not so. She always wanted to be first. And since she was louder, he learned to wait for his turn. And it shaped his character, although now at age four, he's standing up for his rights as boldly and loudly as his sister whilst maintaining his gentle and loving character. I just adore cuddling him as he wraps his little arms around me and says: "I love you, mummy". It's the most beautiful music to my ears.

Being an only child, I was afraid whether I'd know how to love them both equally. Would I be able to raise them properly to look after each other? Would they learn to respect each other and us, their parents?
Would they turn into spoiled brats or would we manage to draw a line between providing them with what they need and offering them a good life and everything we could afford to give them?

Luna and Luka opened up a completely different, wonderful new world to me, a world in which I was free to be myself, to show my true emotions and true love. And I got it back, unconditionally. So how can one go back and forth between this wonderland on one hand and the sometimes heartless, cruel business world on the other? Nobody warned me of the gap I'd encounter between both worlds. Two months before Luka's second birthday, the gap widened even further.

It was Friday afternoon and Luka started vomiting, crying, and showing me that his tummy hurt – this carried on throughout the night. Aco and I took turns to walk around with him as he just couldn't seem to find a comfortable position in his bed. In the morning we took him to the emergency room, but they sent us home saying it was nothing, that he must've eaten something or it was just a virus that would pass. But it didn't. The situation was getting worse and worse by the hour. He was crying all the time, only that now there was nothing left to throw up. I noticed this yellowish liquid coming out of his mouth and decided to take him back to the emergency room. I demanded to be transferred to the hospital. As Luka's health had been very unstable in the first year of his life, we'd spent quite some time in hospitals. In that period I learned to listen and trust my intuition, not to take no for an answer, which in the past had prevented things from going from bad to worse a few times. Luckily, the doctor agreed.

Aco drove us to the hospital. It took the whole day to do various lab tests, ultrasounds etc. but they were still unable to tell me anything about the cause of his condition. Luka was tired from the pain and was constantly half asleep. He was given an intravenous infusion, but couldn't lie down in bed because it was obviously uncomfortable, so I carried him around in my arms most of the day. I was exhausted. By the evening, they told me there was something going on in his tummy, but wouldn't reveal any details. I was scared about what the night would bring; we didn't get any sleep and Luka was vomiting over and over again. The nurse was quite unfriendly, almost hostile because I rang so many times. I was covered in vomit, he was sweating. I wanted to change him, but couldn't do it by myself because of the intravenous needle, and the night nurse wouldn't help me – she barked at me that she had more important things to do than that, and left. We were both crying. I couldn't wait for morning to come.

After another sleepless night, early in the morning I noticed that, while throwing up, something dark brown came out of his mouth. I thought it was blood and rang again, asking the nurse to call the doctor. The nurse refused and asked me to wait for two hours until the regular shift started. I just couldn't bear it any longer, I just couldn't watch my little boy suffer anymore. With tears pouring down my face, I started screaming and demanded someone take a look at my little boy immediately!

I was clearly convincing enough so she reluctantly left to wake the doctor up. After seeing Luka and the scene, the doctor turned around straight away and ran out of the hospital room. A short time later, she returned with three doctors: a gastro specialist, a surgeon, and an anesthesiologist. It was an emergency.

I was carrying his hot, almost lifeless, tiny body around the room paying attention to every weak breath and sound coming from him. The tears were streaming down my face as I called upon God and asked him to save my little boy.

I laid him on the bed. Four of them were hovered over his little body, whispering to each other. I couldn't hear what they were saying as my mind was filled with all kinds of horrible thoughts. What was wrong with him? Why won't they tell me anything?

The next thing I remember was the surgeon's poker face pointing to his swollen belly, telling me where he was going to make a cut and what he was going to do. I broke down.

What if we were to lose him? He's not even two. I felt guilty for all the afternoons I had been in the office instead of being with him, for all the evenings I didn't put him to bed since I had to work. I thought of all the things I could've taught him, but I hadn't. Would I ever get a second chance?

They came to the conclusion that due to his past respiratory problems it'd be best to transfer him to the pediatric division of the University Medical Centre in Ljubljana, where he'd be better taken care of. I don't remember much of the one hour ambulance race to Ljubljana. I was holding his little hand, with my head empty and my soul crying.

He was treated for a very rare gastrointestinal disorder that only 2% of the world population has. The doctor, a surgeon, was very realistic, but at the same time showed a great deal of empathy. His attitude and staff at the clinic improved my overall impression and experience I'd had with health institutions so far. They made me believe everything would work out fine. I needed that badly as every look at my little boy, lying in his little bed, was a struggle – I could hardly hold the tears back.

But it was not the end of the story. Because the wound wouldn't heal for weeks, we saw the last hope in the biotherapist. Enver, who I trusted more than anyone, was very sick at the time, so we asked for an appointment with Zdenko Domančič, the world renowned biotherapist and healer, whose method has also been a frequent subject of scientific tests, shows, movies, interviews, and so on. Due to our boy's serious condition, we got an appointment immediately. After four days of therapy, his condition started to improve, until he was safe and sound. A huge burden was removed from our shoulders.

The whole experience had an important impact on my future. A few months later, Aco and I joined master Domančič and his team to take a level-one course in biotherapy to be able to help our children and family members when in need. We've been practicing it ever since.

At the same time, a new battle was forming in my head. Comparing what doctors and Domančič were doing with what I was doing for a living, I felt empty. How can helping someone to sell more products and make more profit even compare with saving lives? I played with this question a lot.

When Luka was well again, my days were back to normal. The work was piling up, and so too was the stress. It was one of the busiest years in the history of our company.

On the other hand, there were beautiful family moments I didn't know how to enjoy because my mind was too occupied with work issues and challenges. Even when we went for a walk, my mind was always at work. It was impossible for me to switch off. Or better: I didn't know how to do it. I was being dragged into a vicious circle, which was quite frankly making a nagging bitch out of me; turning me into someone I didn't want to become.

KEY TAKEAWAYS:

- Trust your intuition, your gut feeling. It's your inner voice, telling you what is or isn't good for you, and it always knows what's best for you.
- Never settle with anything less then what's best for you, your child, your family, your company, or your business.
- Don't be afraid to look for alternatives, even if that means going against the flow.

LIFE IS NOT ABOUT WAITING
FOR THE STORM TO PASS,
IT'S ABOUT LEARNING HOW TO
DANCE IN THE RAIN.

9. HITTING ROCK BOTTOM

Bit by bit, I began to disappear. I was stuck in a daily routine and the pressure at work to meet deadlines, manage processes and people so everything would run smoothly, deal with clients who didn't respect our time nor our work and were only putting more pressure on us... and, to top it all off, in the evening I slipped into the role of mother and housewife. I didn't realize how exhausted I was until it hit me.

Having your own company, being your own boss sounds great to most outsiders, especially those who've never tried it themselves. You can take a day off anytime you want, you can do whatever you want, and you can take holidays whenever you want to... Yes, great. But that's only one side of the story. Clients become your bosses: they tell you what they want and when they want it. If you look at it from that perspective, all of a sudden you have a dozen bosses who want something from you. And usually they all want it NOW. On the other hand, there's a team of people you work with who rely on you to provide their salaries and keep them motivated every day so they give and perform at their best. You're responsible for maintaining a win-win situation: happy, motivated employees on one hand and a happy client on the other.

Thanks to the great results our clients achieved with our help, they recommended us to their partners. We were very busy, working almost round the clock. There were situations where we had to say no to a new client because we didn't want to jeopardize our 3Rs formula: respect for client and employees, responsibility for the job, and focus on results.

Every time I said 'no' to a potential client, I felt bad. The memory of my father losing his job and us having to make ends meet with only a fraction of what we had before was still fresh in my mind. At that time, I had taken every opportunity for work. While my colleagues were enjoying summer vacations, I was working two shifts: one in the local bank and another in a nearby boutique. I gave English tutoring to students, worked as a translator – anything to make me independent so I wouldn't be a burden on my parents. In this period I promised myself I'd always keep more doors to abundance open.

So when we got a new client, we put in all our efforts to develop a solid long-term relationship with them. Of course, there were projects we did for money and those I did for my soul – I knew in advance we wouldn't earn anything, but I took it on anyway if I liked the people or the company, the product or it was a personal challenge for me. These were the most dangerous ones as they easily dragged me into devoting even more of my attention and time than I initially planned.

The fact was that for me it was extremely difficult to say 'no', even when I knew a potential client just didn't fit our ideal client profile or if they only had a small budget – I wanted to help them all.

We were a great team and business was good. That year, our annual turnover more than doubled compared to the year before. There was a lot of work, all for great clients and challenging projects. I really loved my job so I was easily dr_ workaholic routine. There were days I com_ time. I worked late, came home, put the kids _ not even that), and went back to work. Duri__ little or almost no time with my family. I had no time __ to my children. I had no time for my partner or my friends. _ _ no hobbies, let alone any time for them. The guilt I felt was killing me. On top of that, I was surrounded by the same people all the time. The truth was I had no life.

It slowly started affecting my health. I was becoming tired. I spoke with no one about how I felt, I kept it to myself. I didn't want anyone to get a sense of my weakness, my vulnerability. A new project here and there lifted my spirits and put adrenaline back into my veins. Survival mode.

We started making bold plans for the following year and were way in over our head with them. By the end of the year, I was worn out completely. I was constantly anxious, a new email in my inbox or a phone call was enough to make me feel stressed. I was nervous, barking at my colleagues and family for no obvious reason. I noticed that nobody enjoyed my company, I even sensed they were starting to avoid me. I was on the verge of tears over small stuff like somebody asking me for help. I felt tired all the time. I just couldn't cope with everything any longer. I had a feeling of being torn in two – my job pulling me one way and my family the other. There were all the signs of burnout syndrome.

I spent the whole of December at home, feeling sorry for myself and at the same time angry because I had let myself get sucked in by work so deeply again. I was a living zombie. Nobody knew what was going on, except Aco. Officially I had the flu. After a month at home, with Aco running the business, our household, and taking care of the kids, after many tears, numerous talks with him, I realized that this was not how I wanted to live my life. I felt like a hamster, running round and round on its wheel, working and getting tired, but not really getting anywhere.

knew I had to let go of this lifestyle, but just didn't know how. For the first time in my life, I realized I was not going to be able to do it by myself. I admitted I needed help.

I asked myself a series of questions: what do I need? What kind of life do I want? What's my goal? What's my passion? Where do I see myself in five years?

To my total horror, everything was blank, there were no answers. I didn't have a clue. I felt like I was walking down a dead-end street.

KEY TAKEAWAYS:

- If you think that one day you'll wake up and decide that you want to change – well, you won't. You'll never feel like changing until you experience your own fall.
- Watch out for warning signs of stress – don't wait until you're in the danger zone.
- Recognize the life patterns that come up again and again. What are they telling you?
- Don't blame others for situations.
- Take responsibility for your actions.
- Learn from experiences. Don't replay things over and over.
- Remember: you are NOT your work!

SOMETIMES YOU NEED TO STOP
PUTTING EVERYONE ELSE FIRST
AND JUST DO WHAT'S
BEST FOR YOU.

10. THE TURNING POINT

I had become a service for our clients and for my family. Taking care of everybody's needs, while forgetting about my own, neglecting my talents, my passions. I was feeling stuck in life, hopeless, and frustrated. It started influencing my health: high blood pressure was a warning sign especially since this was the cause of my father's death. It was a wake-up call. I knew I had to do something for myself.

I knew I needed some sort of physical activity – anything to keep me busy and distract my thoughts from everyday life. One day, my sister-in-law Simona saw an ad in a local newspaper for Nia classes – a body, mind, and soul dance class, so we decided to give it a try. Those who know me know that whenever I tried out any kind of sport class I would visit it once or twice, and then give up. I'd tried aerobics, the gym, yoga, running, cycling... the list goes on. While living in Warsaw, I even went to Tai Chi classes a few times but never really enjoyed it. I knew I had to do something for myself, but just couldn't find the motivation to do anything I didn't get pleasure from. For me, it had always been a waste of time, time I could have spent much more wisely, like reading a business article or doing some more work. So my expectations from Nia were really low.

Nia caught me by surprise completely. Our Nia teacher was an energetic person, full of positive energy so it was easy to dive into the new experience. As I moved with the music, I lost myself completely. I felt as if all the weight in my shoulders had disappeared, all my thoughts and problems vanished. My emotional state surprisingly shifted. After each class I just felt good, energized, not exhausted at all. Yet, surprisingly, I found pleasure in Nia dancing.

Nia became my getaway from my everyday routine and an effective way of reducing stress. I couldn't wait for Tuesdays and Thursdays to step into my Nia space and lose myself completely. So when I received an invitation for a "Weekend getaway for body, mind, and soul" which the Nia teachers had organized, I didn't hesitate. For the first time I decided to spend a weekend on my own, without my family. Well, not completely alone – with 40 other women, mostly total strangers, but with one thing in common: we were all passionate Nia practitioners.

It was a huge step out of my comfort zone and, as it turned out, another important turning point in my life. We spent three days dancing, meditating, and cleansing through gong therapies … Enjoying chatting a lot, away from worries and everyday life. Total relaxation. A new dimension of life opened in front of my eyes: there IS life besides work!

Sandra, one of the event organizers, was an intuitive healer. The leaflet said she uses Theta Healing, a holistic healing technique that directly addresses your subconscious mind to fix the 'bugs in your software'. I became interested when I read that the technique helps you clear your limiting beliefs, live life with positive thoughts and thereby transform your life. Out of curiosity I signed up for an individual session.

Honestly, I had no idea what to expect. During the session I sat on a chair in front of Sandra and chatted with her like an old friend. She asked me questions and I cheerfully talked about my life, my partner, my kids, and my business. Actually, I had a great life, I wouldn't change anything. All was well. Then she asked me a simple question: "Are you happy?"

Her words cut into my heart like a knife. "Of course I am", I replied firmly. But deep in my heart I knew the words didn't match how I felt. There was no way back.

There were lots of other questions that remained unanswered. She put a mirror right in front of me and I didn't like what I saw. I realized I was living a life for my clients, for my company, for my family, for my children, for my friends – for everyone around me except for MYSELF. Where was I in this story? Who was I? What did I really want? The truth was devastating: there was no ME in this story, I had lost myself completely.

At the end of the weekend, I returned home, back to my life that wasn't really mine. I felt like my old life had ended, I just had no idea how to go on. Somewhere in the distance I saw a reflection of a new me, my body, my spirit, and my soul. It was the start of a healing process. I felt things would never be the same again.

The months that followed were very difficult for me. Although in the past, I had been a shoulder to cry on for many people, in both my professional and private life I always seemed to know how to listen to other people's problems, to ask them the right questions and it had always been easy for me to solve other people's problems and give advice, I didn't know how to help myself. Now it was my turn: I had to listen to myself and I just didn't know how to talk to myself. Where to start?

I found the answer in meditations with Sandra and a small group – they became my escape from the outside world. I learned to disconnect from my ego and move into a world we don't see. It was initially difficult as my mind often wandered around and tried to dominate the spirit. There were days when I just couldn't switch my mind off. I had to learn to disconnect from my ego that was guiding my life instead of me, telling me what I should and shouldn't do. With practice I learned to quieten down my noisy, always busy mind. I learned to just let be and tune in to the other state of awareness. Into the world we don't see, but which influences our material world.

It was 'me time', during which I realized how disconnected I was from myself and my desires. I didn't know myself at all as my ego was dominating my life. On one occasion, I ran out of the room in the middle of group meditation – I just couldn't bear all the feelings that had started surfacing. So many feelings and memories were buried deep inside my unconscious mind. For decades I had been ignoring them and hadn't dared to face them. There were lots of limiting unhealthy patterns I'd developed over the years that were running my life. I became aware of my self-destructive behavior and limiting beliefs that had been programmed into me by my parents, teachers, culture, society, and the media. By becoming aware of them, I had taken my first step towards healing and I was happy about it.

I enjoyed my conversations with Sandra, our intuitive teacher, who was leading our meditation classes. She used a special technique called Theta meditation to put ourselves into a theta brainwave state and then assist us in transforming our emotions, beliefs, and energies that were contributing to our current imbalance. I enjoyed the process, especially the results it brought, so I took a course in the Theta Healing meditation technique and spiritual philosophy.

I was even more amazed at how simple, yet effective this training method for mind, body, and spirit really was when I started practicing it on my own. It allowed me to clear limiting beliefs about how I saw myself, the things I was afraid of, and what I was worried about. It changed my focus and taught me to live life with positive thoughts, developing virtues in everything I do.

By learning to listen to myself, I took control of my life back into my hands. During the process (which is a never-ending story, by the way), I learned a lot – not only about myself, but also about other people. Some of them spontaneously disappeared from my life. At the same time, I became closer to people who had been there before, but I simply hadn't noticed them. Also new people came into my life – those who were on the same path of self-discovery as me. At the end of the day, it's the quality of relationships that counts, not the number and status of the people around you.

Nia and everything that happened because of Nia was an eye-opening experience. It revealed a new perspective and showed me how little we know about ourselves and how unaware we are of our capabilities. Once I understood what was going on inside me and knew how to find causes for it, I could process it and consciously deal with it. But although I was more at peace with myself, I didn't seem to be any closer to finding my passion. Deep inside, I just felt that the life I was living still didn't completely fit with who I really am.

CHALLENGES FOR YOU:

■ Answer the following questions – write the answers down on a piece of paper.

Step 1: What are the most upsetting thoughts you have about yourself?

Step 2: How do they make you feel? Describe the feeling.
Step 3: Is this actually true or is it only the way YOU see it? Prove that it's true. Prove that it isn't true.
Step 4: How can you improve your reality? What can you do?

- Do something you've never done before, but you've always wanted to do. Join a dance class, go skydiving or swimming with dolphins, or send an introductory email to someone you've always admired and wanted to meet.

- Go out and meet new people. Talk to them, listen to them – everyone is there for a reason, to teach you something.

- Don't be afraid to ask for help. All highly successful people had mentors in earlier stages of their lives.

YOU AND I, WE ALL ARE
SEEKING THE HIGHEST,
TRUEST EXPRESSION
OF OURSELVES AS HUMAN BEINGS.

— OPRAH WINFREY —

11. PERSONAL MISSION

I felt like something was tearing me apart. The feeling of guilt as I thought of my 6-year-old daughter and 4-year-old son was devastating. I didn't want someone else to take care of them, play with them, help them with their homework, read bedtime stories to them while I was at the office. I wanted to be a good mom, but I also loved my job. And secretly, I was longing for more time for myself, me only. Is it possible to balance it all? Above all, I simply wanted to be HAPPY again.

Stop chasing weekends

———

I mostly felt calm and motivated. I spent days at the office or with clients, afternoons with my children, and evenings were reserved for Aco and I. I managed to reduce my stress, my anxiety was gone. However, the challenge of getting back my passion, combining everything I loved and finding my personal mission was still open. I didn't want to force myself into anything, I decided to go with the flow – something would come up sooner or later. It was sooner.

One day while surfing the Internet, I noticed a book about leadership. The topic caught my attention as at the time I was focusing on developing my leadership skills in order to better utilize my strengths and become a better leader. I then realized it was written by Sonja Klopčič, a woman I knew personally – my curiosity was further heightened. I knew there were going to be stories about companies and people I knew pretty well. I immediately ordered the book and started reading it the same day it was delivered to my door.

First and foremost, I expected practical advice on how to manage people more effectively, how to drive their passion, and motivate them to pursue the path Aco and I had envisioned for our company. But, to my surprise, I got much more than that. I recognized myself in the author's story and her struggles. It was a perfect mirror of what I was going through, split between the material world I knew so well on one hand, and the spiritual world that was opening up all around me on the other. I was relieved: phew, ok, I wasn't alone; I wasn't the only one going through the transformation.

After reading the book, I gave Sonja a call. She was surprised to hear me after all these years and more so when, after chatting about the book, I asked her to be my coach. Without hesitation she said yes and so we set up our first meeting.

I was really nervous about meeting her in person after all this time. It had been 24 years since I had worked for her company as a young student. What if she didn't have all the answers? What if I'm unable to take a step forward? What if...??? My head was spinning with all kinds of questions.

My life was not that bad after all; maybe I should just cancel the meeting. If I had lived without help until now, I'd bring around myself again. Yes, all kinds of thoughts were running through my mind. Thank god my fears and insecurities didn't stop me.

So there I was, sitting in front of her, expecting her to bring out a magic wand and – puff! – have all the answers for me at once. Well, it wasn't anything close to that. First, she asked me why I was there, what my challenges were. I honestly told her the whole story: how I lived and what my struggles were. I said that so far I had managed to fulfill all my dreams; I'd reached all my goals, personal and professional. And that on the way I'd somehow lost myself, so I didn't find passion in anything I was doing anymore. My attention was scattered across a lot of different, seemingly unrelated things. How do I combine my multiple strengths and talents with what I like and enjoy doing?

On the outside, my life was great. I had a beautiful family, two gorgeous healthy kids, a loving man who adored me, good friends, family that gave me support, a warm home, a cozy life but, nevertheless, I felt empty inside.

I told her about our company and its reference list that contained all the big and important clients' logos I was once dreaming about. I had a good reputation in professional networks. Even the fact we didn't have to go out searching for new clients anymore because they mostly came through recommendations wasn't making me happy. In the past, I was so passionate about solving clients' challenges, but now not even the most complex issues satisfied me.

I missed that passion so much! The butterflies in my stomach after winning a new client, the feeling of victory when a problem was solved, the satisfaction when goals were met. You know, the feeling that makes you want to get out of bed in the morning. I wanted my passion back!

Sonja listened to me and calmed me down: "everything's fine, we just need to find your personal mission". I had no idea what she was talking about. She explained that a personal mission statement provides clarity and gives you a sense of purpose. It defines who you are and how you'll live.

She took me through an exercise by asking four simple questions. Yet, for me, these were the most difficult questions anyone had ever asked me! I sweated a lot, my brain was working overtime and, by the end, my personal mission statement was written out on a piece of paper. And I was happy like a little kid. Yes!

It combined both worlds: business and personal. The simple statement said more about me than I could write in a book. It said:

"I empower people to bring out the best in themselves and bridge the gap between where they are in life and where they want to be."

It was just perfect! It could be applied to everything I am and do: my private life, my job, relationships with my friends and business partners. It highlighted my attributes and everything I wanted to be: finding the best in others, (people, products, or companies) and bringing it out in a way so that others can also see it.

I already do that at work by creating stories and new business opportunities for companies and brands, during training by teaching people new skills and thereby empowering and motivating them, and in my private life by helping family and friends develop a positive perspective on a situation and helping them grow through that.

I finally had my personal mission statement that I could build my life around.

A CHALLENGE FOR YOU:

DISCOVER YOUR PERSONAL MISSION

Find yourself somewhere peaceful. Take a notebook and a pen (a computer can also be used, but I'm more fond of handwriting as all the emotions and creativity come out of me when I scribble on a piece of paper).

Step 1:
Think about all your STRENGTHS, positive attributes, values, what are you good at, what you think is BEST about you, what are you BEST at. Thoroughly write a bullet-point list of everything that comes to your mind. When you're finished, go through all the points and pick (underline) one that is the most important to yo. Underline that word, so you can clearly see it.

Step 2:
Think about how others see you. What do THEY think about you? Write down a few sentences about what your friends or colleagues at work might say or feel about you.

Step 3:
What do you bring into a team? What happens when you join a team?

Step 4:
What would you like others to think about you when they first meet you? How would you like to be introduced?

WHEREVER YOU ARE,
AT WHATEVER AGE,
YOU ARE ONLY
A THOUGHT AWAY
FROM CHANGING YOUR LIFE.

— WAYNE W. DYER —

12. MAKE
YOUR OWN RULES

Finding the best in people and products, and bringing it out in a way others can see it too is my day-to-day reality. Achieving sales and marketing goals. Meeting deadlines. Working long hours. Driving from one place to another, spending hours in the car. Taking care of the kids. Exceeding others' expectations. Not anymore. I've had enough.

In the past, I thought the more projects or clients I could manage simultaneously, the more appreciated I'd be – until I realized I had too many doors open and I mostly felt like I was trapped in a cage.

I never switched off. While playing with the kids, my mind often wandered away. Physically I was present in the room, but mentally I was far away. Even when we went out for a walk, I took it as an opportunity to think about projects and maybe get a new, fresh idea. I didn't know how to take a break. How to switch off. There was no off-work time. My brain was always on standby.

It's frustrating when you feel there is part of you inside that wants to escape, but just can't find its way out. It doesn't know how to. I realized that if I wanted to make my dreams a reality, I'd just have to close those doors that didn't lead to my goals.

First, I made some changes at work. We mapped all the internal processes: client acquisition, creative processes, production, administration etc. We divided them into phases or steps, and then assigned each step to an individual responsible for it. We took a closer look at it and then optimized the processes so the internal resources would be used wisely, with each person performing the task they are most capable of, and at the same time optimizing the time and resources required to perform each task.

Each of us made a list of all the tasks we carried out daily. We reassigned some tasks to better fit with the employee skills or put them on an 'outsource' list. I was more than happy to mark all my tasks that could be delegated to my colleagues so I could get rid of the excess work that was creating a lot of stress for me, causing a bottleneck. At the same time, my colleagues were given greater autonomy and responsibility.

We all agreed that also in the future we would focus only on what we did best and find ideal clients. We defined the ideal client profile, but at the same time made it very clear what kind of clients don't fit into our picture.

We continued cooperating with those who respected us, our work, and shared our values. I strongly believe that if we want to be successful in what we do, there has to be trust, respect and some magic, chemistry between both teams, our clients' and ours – it's so much more enjoyable to co-create in such an environment.

In the past, the fear of saying 'no' to a prospective client had brought in some projects that were consuming a lot of our time, but provided no real value. We said goodbye to a few clients and, by doing so, made room for the new ones that match our vision. We focused on our core competencies and decided to outsource everything that didn't fit into the main frame. When we finished with all those changes, I was relieved.

An important part of the change process was applying the changes to my daily routine. Now it was time to dig a bit deeper. I started writing down how I spent my time. Hour by hour, day after day. What I did at work and how I spent my afternoons, evenings, and weekends. The results were devastating. I realized that most of my time was devoted to work: to projects, 'to do' lists, potential clients, business development. This had to change.

I started reading articles and books about time management and made an implementation plan for applying changes to my daily routine. I was obsessed with optimizing my time, setting deadlines, dividing work, and delegating tasks.
As a result, I became more organized at work: at the end of each day, I prepared a daily 'to do' list for the following day. The task I hated most was always at the top of the 'to do' list. I realized that, once I got that out of the way, everything else seemed to be done easily, with no effort.

At the beginning, there were too many tasks on my daily 'to do' list. I learned to keep it short and realistic so at the end of the day I wouldn't feel overwhelmed by looking at the list of unfinished tasks that had to be postponed to the next day. It helped me to stay focused on what's important and take one task at a time, rather than scatter my attention over plenty of minor ones.

Before, I used to stay in the office until evening. There was always something to do. I stopped working overtime and left the office by 5 p.m. at the latest. The funny thing is that, even though I spent less time at the office, I was more productive and did more than I had done previously. It helped to apply creative thinking techniques to processes, like Edward de Bono's six thinking hats for example – it helped our team and I organize our thoughts – the outcomes were amazing. We became more effective, generated more and better ideas and improved our cooperation as a team.

I have also redesigned my working week: I spend Mondays and Fridays in the office, Tuesdays, Wednesday, and Thursdays I'm out of the office with our clients or at meetings. I rarely make an exception to that, knowing that it'd quickly lead me back to my old vicious circle. Phone calls to or from clients are taken from 9 a.m. to 5 p.m. and, no matter how smart my mobile phone is, I check and reply to emails during the same time, on workdays only. I can say that I'm in control of my time.

And the best of it: by applying the new routine to my daily itinerary I actually ended up with more time for myself and everything I loved. I never miss my Nia class, an hour stolen for myself in the evening twice a week. I spend more afternoons with my kids, playing with them, going for walks, cycling or simply hanging out with them and enjoying our company.

It's amazing to see how these small changes improved the quality of my life, my relationships with the people around me, especially Aco and my children, and the quality of our life as a family. It doesn't have to be Sunday anymore to drive down to the coast and go for a walk by the seaside – now any day can be a 'weekend'.

Isn't that funny? Everything I ever wanted was already there. All I had to do was to put my priorities straight to realize how and who I wanted to spend my time with and what I didn't want in my life anymore. It was all just a matter of changing perspective, reorganizing priorities, and better time management. I felt fulfilled and happy.

A CHALLENGE FOR YOU:

Step 1:
Take a closer look at how you spend your life. What occupies you most? What do you focus on most?

Step 2:
Create a vision: if today was your last day on Earth, what would you do? What would you like to spend more time on?

Step 3:
Get your goals and priorities straight.

Step 4:
Take action:

- Record how you spend your time, day by day, hour by hour. Analyze it.
- Reorganize your daily routine. Make a daily task plan and stick to it.
- Get rid of the tasks that don't bring you any closer to your goal.
- Create space for working on your goal or dream. Over time, you'll see that ever more space is available to support you in your efforts.

THE ONLY LIMITS IN LIFE ARE THE ONES YOU SET FOR YOURSELF.

— WAYNE W. DYER —

13. BELIEVE IN YOURSELF

If someone told me to describe myself in three words, I'd probably have great difficulty since I play so many roles during the day that it'd be hard to narrow it down to just three. I'm a mother, a wife, a lover, a house-wife, a cleaning lady, a stylist, a cook, a mediator, a trip planner, an entertainer, 'Wikipedia' on two legs, a household manager, a driver, a dancer, a singer, a piano player, an entrepreneur, a writer, a friend, a motivator, a coach, a speaker, a Theta Healing intuitive practitioner, a biotherapist, … hmmm, I'm sure I've forgotten something.

We all perform different roles in our lives. But all too often our self-esteem and self-worth boils down to what we do for a living. Our occupation, our work; how much we earn and the material things we possess.

For the last 24 years I have lived in some kind of spotlight: either as a marketing manager, waiting for the response of consumers to prove whether our marketing strategy was successful, in the role of a public speaker at marketing events and conferences,

Stop chasing weekends

as a trainer and coach for our company's or clients' employees, helping them to improve their marketing, sales, and communication skills, even as a guest professor at one of the colleges.

But no matter how many times I stood in front of an audience, I always had butterflies in my stomach. Would I be good enough? What would they think of me? Why didn't I ... Maybe I should have ... It's amazing how easily we find positive and kind words of praise for our children, our friends, our colleagues at work, even total strangers whereas we can be hard on ourselves, sometimes even cold-hearted and cruel. The problem is that if we keep repeating negative thoughts about ourselves over and over again in our heads, they become a reality.

I was so full of self-doubt and occupied with what others thought of me that sometimes I forgot about the most important thing: to just be MYSELF. In the search for that passionate girl inside me I came to the point where I really didn't know who I was anymore. Yet, as soon as I started throwing away all the clutter and limiting beliefs from my subconscious and set my priorities straight, the picture became clearer. Now I just wanted to see how my newly found personal mission fit with how others were seeing me.

While having lunch with my good friend Barbara, I surprised her with a question: "why are you my friend?" She looked at me in disbelief, like "why the hell are you asking me that", and then I saw her face change as she was thinking about what I had just asked her. And finally she answered: because you make me feel good about myself. Hmmm. I liked what I heard.

I repeated the same exercise with another friend, a person I grew up with and who has known me since childhood, who always knew my darkest thoughts and deepest secrets. Even though we live 150 km apart and talk every once in a while, we seem to be connected on a higher level. We seem to feel how the other feels, when it's the right time to call, what needs to be said without even asking what is going on. It just feels so natural with her. During one of our phone chats, I popped the same question: "Why are you my friend?" She answered without hesitation: "Because you're my soulmate". "True," I agreed.

Yes, I learned long ago that there are people in life who cross our path and stay forever. And there are those who cross our path and vanish and we don't even notice. And, finally, there is Aco, the love of my life, the person who knows me inside and out. So he was the last on the list. "Why are you with me?" I asked him one evening. His answer was straightforward: "Because you're the way you are." I smiled at him, and felt loved. I'm so lucky to have a man who loves me for who I am. I'm blessed.

The truth is it's perfectly ok to be ME. People like me because of me. We all wear masks in our everyday lives to protect ourselves from being hurt; we pretend to be bold, strong, and marvelous. However, in each and every one of us there's a child, a little girl with her fears, her negative thoughts and limiting beliefs about herself, with memories and experiences that constrain her in some way and shape the way she reacts to the situations life brings her. What we are and what we're not, what we can or cannot, or should or should not do....

I learned I don't have to be anyone else but me. I'm enough. Everything is right, as it should be. Now I know that I'm perfect just the way I am, with all my imperfections. That I can allow myself to be weak. To cry and ask for help. To be sad. To be gentle and loving. To be crazy. To dream with my eyes wide open. To be MYSELF. To set that little girl inside me free. To live my life and do things my way. Because there's no point in doing what I'm doing if I'm not having fun along the way.

A CHALLENGE FOR YOU:

■ Describe your life in one word. How does that make you feel?

■ Which specific situations trigger your self-doubt? Understand the causes of your self-doubt. Go out there and get the training you need or find someone who has experience with it and can help you. Anything can be learned.

■ **Write a letter to yourself.**
Choose a quiet, private place. Take a few minutes just for yourself. Put on some relaxation music and quieten down your mind. Look into your heart.

What would you like to say to yourself, to tell or confess to yourself? What are your needs? How do you feel? What do you love about yourself? Why do you admire yourself? What do you respect yourself for? What are your hopes and dreams? What do you wish for yourself?

Write the letter on a piece of paper and put it in an envelope. Put the sealed envelope in a hidden place. It'll come into your hands just at the right time. You'll be amazed once you find it again as it brings you love and hope and the belief you can overcome everything, how strong you are and that you're loved.

FRIENDSHIP ISN'T ABOUT WHO YOU'VE KNOWN THE LONGEST... IT'S ABOUT WHO CAME AND **NEVER LEFT YOUR SIDE.**

14. FRIENDS AND SOULMATES

We parked behind the building, gently took our things out and moved towards the back entrance so she wouldn't see us. Girls from other cities were already waiting. We quickly changed into our dance clothes and quietly waited in front of the ballroom, feeling like naughty little girls, doing something we shouldn't be doing. At 7.30 p.m. we knocked on the door and entered: "Is this where the party is?"

Mateja is the soul of the Nia movement in our country and the person who brought Nia to Slovenia. I had a few occasions to dance with her, which all turned out to be eye-opening experiences. She always inspired us to open our hearts, taught us to listen to our bodies, to love life, and encouraged us to spread our wings and fly. It's true; dancers don't need wings to fly.

When I first met her, I was amazed at the elegance and ease with which she danced and moved her body to the rhythm of the music. She easily connected with everyone on the floor and thus created a beautiful energy in the room. She appeared so gentle, her feminine side expressing goodness and fragility. She was completely the opposite of me – like yin and yang.

We all have a masculine and feminine side, regardless of our gender: the feminine side expressing empathy and the need to show emotions, and the masculine side focusing on power and the ability to achieve goals. We need a balance of both, yet most of us tend to have a dominant side.

And if Mateja was more 'yin', then I was more 'yang', expressing strength, while trying to hide my feminine side – it just didn't go along with the role I had been used to playing all my life.

That's also why I didn't like Mateja's classes at first: I had a problem relaxing and expressing myself in free dance, I hated physical contact with other dancers. I was uncomfortable to gaze into her or other people's eyes, it was all just too personal for me. But during my encounters with her I realized why she made me feel uncomfortable. She was actually showing me the side of myself I didn't want to see, the side I was trying to hide and was afraid to expose to the outside world: my feminine side, my fragility, vulnerability, my emotions.

She helped me bring out the woman inside me, taught me I don't have to be strong and invincible all the time, that it is ok to be weak, that it is ok to show emotions. The beauty lies in what or who we ARE and I'm so grateful to her for showing me this. When I made this realization, I started enjoying classes with her even more.

Her birthday was soon approaching so at the next Nia class I suggested organizing a surprise visit to one of her classes. Our teacher thought it was a great idea and promised to check it out with teachers from other cities. They all agreed. The plan was to get there secretly and 'bump' into her regular class.

When we opened the door, she just stood there and stared at us with disbelief, probably asking herself "what on earth is going on?" But then it dawned on her and a big smile spread across her face. Yes, WE were her birthday surprise. The hour that followed was one of the most beautiful Nia classes I had ever been to. Yes, Nia has brought some great people into my life and some of them have become my close friends – I'm so grateful.

I'm also grateful for my dearest childhood friends; after 38 years, they are still an important part of my life and in my circle of trust. Even though we only see each other a few times a year, have totally different lifestyles and paces of life, when we meet, it feels like yesterday. Nothing's changed between us.

As children, we used to live in the same building in the days when there were no computers or mobile phones. Afternoons were mostly spent outside, running around, giving neighbors, who didn't like the noise of screaming children, a hard time, riding bikes or playing hide & seek. Together, we explored the secrets of growing up, sharing experiences with first boyfriends, laughing together when things went well, and offering each other a shoulder to cry on when needed.

Every December we organize a 'girls' night out'. It's an emotional get-together that lasts long into the night. We just have to catch up on what's happened in the past year. We bring up memories and talk about good old times and laugh a lot. We discuss 'life challenges' we have in front of us (you know, more heads, more solutions). After all these years, we still have much to talk about.

No matter where we meet, whether it is pampering in a spa, a workshop with a make-up artist, or just a fine dinner (oh yes, we know how to pamper ourselves) – at the end of the day, it doesn't really matter to us where we are. All that matters is the time we spend together.

We don't have to pretend to be something we're not. We know

each other inside out. The longer we know each other, the closer we are and the more we respect each other. We're friends for who we really are and not for what we possess or what we have become. We are friends forever.

Do I have a lot of friends? Due to the nature of my work I know many people, but the door to my home or even my heart is open to only a few very special ones. There are very few people I share my most intimate moments and thoughts with. With some of them I have a special, almost telepathic connection – I feel they can almost read my mind. It doesn't really matter whether we've just met or we've known each other for ages – with some people you just click from the very first moment.

Yes, there are people who come into our lives and leave a lasting impact. Some of them come and stay forever; others leave when there's nothing left to say. And there are people who hop on and off the train of life as it takes us to our final destination. They always come at the right time, with the right message. We need them all because, if we open our hearts, we can learn from each and every one of them.

As my mom told me when I was little: "You can't call everyone 'a friend'. Friends are very special people and friendship's a very special and rare gift you have to nourish. It's delicate like a bubble and precious like a diamond."

I'm so happy and thankful to have you in my life, my dear friends. You're so SPECIAL and BEAUTIFUL, inside and out. You've always been there for me and I know I can always count on you. I hope you know you can always count on me, too. ALWAYS.

A CHALLENGE FOR YOU:

1. Think about your friends. Who are they, what do they mean to you?
2. How much time do you devote to them?
3. What can you do to make them, or one of them, happy? What can you do TODAY? Sometimes just a phone call will do, an hour spent together or a quick coffee taken during working hours.

YOU ARE RICH,
WHEN YOU ARE CONTENT
AND HAPPY WITH
WHAT YOU HAVE.

15. BE GRATEFUL

We visited some good friends who live in a tiny, but very neatly furnished and smartly organized house. You see straightaway how the owners have creatively used the limited space. They found countless options to recycle, refurnish, refurbish, and recolor the furniture to make it look new and modern again. I doubt whether top interior designers would've been able to think of a smarter way to reuse old furniture parts and pieces and organize the space in a better way to meet the family's living and storage needs. It felt like home.

———

We don't see each other often, but whenever we visit them we always feel at home. The tiny, furniture-filled living room leaves little space for us to move and becomes even more crowded when we all squeeze in to catch up on everything that has happened since we last saw each other. Everything that can't be said through Facebook, Skype, Viber, or phone. It just feels different to be in the same room, to feel the energy, to see the faces and their reactions when you talk to them and laugh together. I just love them all.

No matter how modestly they live, their dignity is intact. They're proud of who they are. They've learned to survive, to live day by day and to make ends meet with what they have. They learned to be very creative in recycling everything: from furniture, clothes, even food. And although they don't have much, they're happy. Moreover, they're willing to share what they have with anyone who comes along. And their house is always full.

By spending a day with them, you can clearly see how much they appreciate the small things. How they enjoy each day, how they value and appreciate every moment they spend with each other.

They cherish what they have, and each other. They take time to sit down and talk to each other. They find time to meet with friends for a coffee in person. They know their neighbors by name and call them 'friends'. Family members aren't strangers to each other. They haven't allowed the stressful pace of modern life and technology to conquer their world.

I'm not sure if they realize how lucky they are. I only know that I realized what we've long lost in our modern society and are now trying hard to rebuild again; the ties, the bonds between us, relationships with friends and family, the feeling of belonging, the dignity of being who you are. Accepting people for who they are and not for what they have. The quality of relationships with people we care for and respect and who care for and respect us.

Spending time with them made me realize there's a lot in my life to be thankful for. First of all, I'm grateful for who I am, for my life, my health. I'm grateful to my parents for bringing me up to be the person I am today, for believing in me and showing me I had wings to fly, for teaching me to respect everyone regardless of who they are or what they do for a living, to respect even those who don't respect me, not to lower my integrity for anyone.

I'm grateful that every day I wake up with the man that I love and who loves me. I'm grateful for having wonderful kids, who challenge me every day to become a better person and a mom as they mirror my behavior and actions. I'm grateful for all my friends for all the laughs and cries we have together, especially for those who have stuck by me since we were kids.

I'm grateful for all my teachers, who always came along at the time I needed them.
I'm grateful for all the adventures and opportunities life has offered me, for all the talents I took for granted for so long and for all the experience, ups and downs, good or bad, which made me who I am. And even if sometimes I felt lost – it was just my way of reaching out for help and an opportunity for taking a step forward to become a better version of myself. And I'm grateful for that.

Being grateful reminds me how enriched I am and how loved I am. Because at the end of the day, love is all that really matters. And I learned to love myself and enjoy my life as me and not what the world wants me to be.

A CHALLENGE FOR YOU:

EVERY MORNING REMIND YOURSELF WHAT YOU'RE GRATE-FUL FOR.

Write it down on a piece of paper or in your diary – whatever suits you best. Focus on positive things that happen, on what you love, all the good in your life. Embrace the sun and the rain, the ups and downs, all the experiences and people that have made you who you are today. Remind yourself how smart and beautiful you are, for this helped you become who you are. Remind yourself of your beauty, because it makes you shine like no one else, and your achievements because it's YOU and only YOU who has achieved this so far. Remain open for miracles that are coming your way.

EVERYTHING IS ENERGY AND
THAT'S ALL THERE IS TO IT.
MATCH THE FREQUENCY OF THE
REALITY YOU WANT AND YOU CANNOT
HELP BUT GET THAT REALITY.
IT CAN BE NO OTHER WAY.
THIS IS NOT PHILOSOPHY.
THIS IS PHYSICS.

— ALBERT EINSTEIN —

16. GET YOUR HAMSTER

Everyone has dreams. Wishes we want to come true. Hopes to be fulfilled. Goals to be reached. But sometimes the fear of failure is too strong and we don't even try. We become victims of our own past experiences and let them drag us down. It's easy to let circumstances and self-doubt sabotage our endeavors. And because we're afraid to take a step forward, to step outside our comfort zone, nothing really happens. Luckily, children don't have self-limiting beliefs – here's an excellent example I learned a lot from.

"I want a hamster!", proclaimed my 6-year-old daughter one day after coming home from school. "A what?", I asked in disbelief. "A hamster", she replied very firmly. It seemed obvious that her mind had already been made up and that the topic was not a matter for discussion. However, I'm not that easily walked over. At least, I want some room for negotiation (or at least the impression that I have some).

After all, it really wouldn't be such a drama to have a small hamster besides a dog, a dozen hens, a rooster and two sheep (two pigs have just recently gone to heaven – may they rest in peace). So I started.

"Why do you want a hamster?", I asked. "Oh, he's sooo cute, I saw him on YouTube. I'd love to take care of him. I'll feed him; bring him water, clean up after him. I'll play with him and he also plays by himself – you know, they love pipes and tunnels and … I don't think there's any need to explain how long the list in favor of HAMSTER was… "So, mummy, what do you think?"

"Look, I really wouldn't want to have another animal in the house. Aki[1] is more than enough. Have you talked to daddy? I think we all need to agree on having another family member before we buy one."

"He said yes and Luka also agrees," she replied firmly. Hmmm, I wasn't quite sure about the honesty of that statement, so I checked with Aco just in case. No, I wasn't wrong. He thought he said 'no', but the way she twisted him around her little finger meant he had (once again) fallen into her trap. She asked if she could have a hamster for her birthday (not just any day) and he said something like "we'll see and talk about it" – it was still 8 months away! Ok, she created a good reason to buy her one.

However, I still didn't want to give up and so I reinforced my arguments. For a while, it seemed she had accepted the fact we all needed to agree before getting a hamster.

As a smart 6-year-old girl, the next day she started applying the pressure. "Mummy, what color hamster would you prefer: white, brown, or black?"

Hmmm, smart little devil, now it was not 'yes' or 'no', she had already moved on to the next stage, we were already discussing the color!!! "Daddy likes the brown one." (Poor daddy, he's roasted already!!!)

[1] Aki is our family dog.

So now I needed to decide on the color... Great, I still have 8 months till her birthday, I grinned to myself.

The next day I came back from work to find a nice drawing on the kitchen table. It was very colorful and obviously a lot of attention had been paid to the details. She really is a little Picasso; she's loved painting and drawing since she was 2 years old. She's capable of creating all kinds of interesting art objects out of any material, even trash she finds round the house. I'm so proud of her. Yet, there was a little detail on the picture I didn't like.

Among all the details, the tubes, the little bowl with food and another one with water, the playground and wooden shavings there was ... of course, a hamster. It was a perfectly furnished cage with a hamster, brown with white and black marks (I guess just in case we couldn't decide on the color, she had made the decision for us.)

It was the perfect visualization of her wish (so we wouldn't be in doubt when making the purchase). I couldn't help myself, I started laughing. She's made the whole plan, step by step, to get to her goal. Actually, it wasn't a question of whether or not we'd have a hamster anymore, she had cleverly taken a step forward and started selecting the color, the time of delivery and even listed all the hamster accessories needed. A+ girl. For effort, persistence, strategy, and execution. She deserves to get that hamster.

Why am I writing this? Because this is just one of the challenges she throws at me every day that helps me grow. I know she's not aware of that, but I'm very grateful for all the lessons she's given me since she was born.

The hamster challenge caught me at a time when I was in between worlds: the old and the new me. With one foot in the past, one in the future, with the book, but not quite there yet because I was afraid to make the move; I was taught to be 'normal', not to stand out. And the book I had in mind meant standing out. Although in the past 24 years I had written a lot of content for our clients, in a variety of forms, from business articles to brochures, websites, advertisements, even screenplays for TV commercials, it was all about them, not me. If I gathered it all together and published it in book form, I guess it would have filled a nice section of a library. Still, this book's different. It's my story, my experience, and combines the best of my two worlds.

The hamster experience opened my eyes. I put myself in her shoes, analyzed the path and took the same steps. It worked! I created a whole new vision of my personal mission and developed a step-by-step plan to reach it. Now I know what I'll do in the future, how I'll combine what I had been doing for the last 24 years with what I love and enjoy. This book's a small, yet very important piece of the puzzle.

A CHALLENGE FOR YOU:

WHAT'S YOUR DREAM, YOUR WISH, A GOAL YOU WANT TO ACHIEVE?

1. Sit on a comfortable chair. Close your eyes. Make a wish or define a goal. Or think about how you'd like your life to be.
2. Visualize it. Visualize you having it, reaching your goal. Think about how it makes you feel.
3. Describe it in words or draw a picture of it. Talk about it as if it's already there, already happening. Feel the joy, the gratitude. Save the piece of paper for later.
4. Make a plan – how will you get there, step by step.
5. Start taking steps, one by one.
6. When you get stuck, go back to steps 2 and 3. Feel it. Then continue. You can do it. You will do it.

BEAUTY BEGINS THE
MOMENT YOU DECIDE
TO BE YOURSELF.

— COCO CHANEL —

17. THE SECRET TO SUCCESS AND HAPPINESS

There were times when I was full of self-doubt, constantly judging myself, looking for approval of my decisions and actions. As though I was not doing enough or not doing it well enough. I had to learn how to take a step back and reconnect with myself. The gift I got was priceless.

During my years as a workaholic, I had chosen success over my happiness. I confused success with my career, later with my company reputation, reputable clients, publicity and public speaking, branded clothes, savings in my bank account, a house and car parked in front of it, a summer house at the seaside.

Yes, one could say these are all signs of success. I was blinded by the illusion of the material world. I kept searching for happiness in the outside world until I realized I had been looking in all the wrong places. It was all just a manifestation of what I did for a living. It was merely an illusion of happiness. In reality, I wasn't happy with my life, with how I spent most of my time and who or what I devoted it to.

I paid too much attention to the outside world: the opinions of peers, colleagues, and clients, always striving to exceed the expectations of the spectators, like in a theatre, and if I didn't get the applause at the end of the show, I wasn't worth much. Although from the outside I was living a perfect life, I wasn't happy.

I realized that success was not the key to happiness. That being happy was not about being happy at work. That work was only a small part of my life and that, if I wanted to be happy, I had to bring out that girl inside of me.

The secret to success was to acknowledge the need for change and turn it into something that's fun, purposeful, relevant, and engaging. To embrace the challenges with open hands and take a step forward.

The truth is that I never felt like changing and, believe me, you won't either. The fear of the unknown, the comfort of the situation I knew well and the environment so familiar to me and the people I felt cozy with, were too strong a magnet. I became so accustomed to the role I had been playing that it was hard to let it go, leave it behind, or to change it. But life is too short for such compromises. How to start?

At 44, a friend of mine quit her well-paid managerial position, took her child out of school and went with him on an around-the-world trip for a year. What a brave thing to do, to leave everything behind – it takes lots of guts! But is it really necessary to run away to find peace within yourself? The new environment can help, but the fact is that you can't run away from yourself, no matter how far you go.

The outside world is only a reflection of what is going on inside you. It was not until I changed the perspective from which I looked at my life that things started changing. What I was looking for was already there all the time.

Sometimes you need to stop to find the right path, to slow down the pace of life and ask yourself a few simple questions, set your priorities straight, create new goals, and start taking small steps towards them.

So I did it, step by step. By changing my daily routine I reorganized my life, how I spent my time, and who I spent it with. It was not only work anymore: I devoted more time to my family, my partner and children, and I had greater time for what I loved: dancing, reading, walks, and meditation.

At the company, we distributed various tasks: Aco has taken over the company management, finance, and organization, while I focus on business development, marketing, and strategic consulting. I have more time for running workshops and coaching clients' employees on direct marketing and sales communications, occasionally speaking at marketing and business events.

I restructured my workshops so that besides direct sales and marketing techniques they now also include self-empowerment techniques and exercises to help participants re-discover their 'why', to motivate them to become better at what they do. The response I get is amazing. Yes, it has all been worth it. I have started living my personal mission: empowering people by bringing out the best in them.

I noticed that when I started changing, people around me changed as well. Everything just seems to run more smoothly. I spend more time doing things I enjoy, not feeling guilty if I'm not working. I have stopped planning so much: I literally take and live one day at a time, and enjoy each and every moment. I knew all those phrases from before, I just didn't understand what they really meant and was definitely not living accordingly. And, last but not least, I don't take anything for granted anymore.

Now I know that success isn't the key to happiness – on the contrary, happiness is the key to success. I have learned that if I'm not happy on the journey, I won't be happy at the destination. That's why I see no point in doing things I don't enjoy. I know that if I focus on what I love, I'll be successful, no matter what I do.

I'm no longer afraid of making mistakes. They're just an inevitable part of my life, experiences with a purpose to wake me up, showing me to move in another direction. Yes, you either win or you learn. And I'm thankful for all the learnings.

KEY TAKEAWAYS:

- The outside world is only a reflection of what is going on inside of you.
- Success is not a key to happiness - on the contrary, hapiness is the key to success.
- A mistake is not a failure. It's only a lesson to open your eyes and showing you to move in another direction.
- Be grateful for every lesson life offers you.

THE FUTURE BELONGS
TO THOSE WHO
BELIEVE
IN THE BEAUTY OF THEIR DREAMS.

— ELEANOR ROOSEVELT —

18. CHOOSE
A NEW STORY

We were sitting on the floor in a circle, silently holding hands. A group of women. So different from the outside, but so similar on the inside. Each of us with her own little drama going on, her own life story, sorrows, dreams, passions, and longings. There's no single recipe to inner peace, to success, to harmony, to health, to the stars. But we can and should always support each other and give each other the courage to never stop dreaming.

─────

The air was thick, full of love and emotions. A feeling of inner peace and deep love was running through my veins. Here I was, as vulnerable as never before, yet so strong like never before. With an open heart and eyes full of tears I knew the old me was gone. I had discovered my inner power, trust in myself and trust in women.

I closed my eyes and tried to recall every moment of the intensive weekend that was coming to an end. A perfect 'weekend for soul and body' as the organizers had called it. Yet it was so much more than Nia dancing classes, mantras, and meditations. It was a reunion of the mind, body, and soul; a weekend full of self-awareness, sharing, dancing, laughing, and crying, but above all thankfulness for being, existing, and breathing.

It was a get-together of women who believe in the individual and collective power of women; those who believe that personal growth starts with confessing your weaknesses to yourself and dealing with them, with finding limiting beliefs and removing the causes of them, by connecting to the intelligence of our soul, who is never wrong, we just have to learn how to listen to it. The real beauty of life is enjoying the little things; the everyday moments and sparkles we all too often take for granted.

It was also an important step in the quest of the woman inside me. The woman who buried her dreams to be on the safe side, her talents due to her fear of failure, her emotions to prove she was strong. That she can handle everything by herself, without any help. That nothing can hurt her stone-like exterior.

I don't need to wear that mask anymore. I no longer care what others think of me. I don't need anyone's approval. I dare to be who I am and I'm proud of that. I'm enough. I've come a long way and I know there's a long journey still ahead of me. I've learned to enjoy the journey itself. I embrace all lessons on the way to my destination as each experience makes me stronger. And I love the new ME I am discovering.

This is my story, but it could've been anybody's story. There are things in everybody's life we're afraid to admit to ourselves, let alone share with others. I've been there myself. I've walked every step of the way. I've stumbled, fallen, but always got up and kept walking. And it'll definitely happen again. But today I know there are no failures in life: you either win or you learn. And I still learn every day.

For a long time I thought I had to please others. I thought I had to do everything by myself. I learned to ask for help and learn from people who had been there and done it themselves, and not from people who read books and only repeated what they had read about without having experienced it. It was hard at the beginning because I thought asking for help was a sign of weakness. But whenever I asked for help, I always got it. It usually came at the most unusual times, in the most unexpected forms. I have learned that the Universe is always there for me. I have realized things happen for a reason and people cross our paths for a reason.

My spiritual teacher Sandra reminded me many times: "Stop searching for answers on the outside. Everything you need is already inside you. Listen to your heart." And she was right. On this journey I have learned to listen to my heart and to trust myself and my inner voice. It's never let me down since.

This book is a summary of everything I've learned on my way so far. It wasn't easy to share my most intimate thoughts and moments with you. Most of you are total strangers. Well, not anymore. Now you know me inside and out. But now when it's completed, I realize that writing this book was an important part of my healing process, allowing me to truly free myself from my ego, my past, and to start living my life to its fullest. I'm happy.

I'll be happy if my story empowers you to take the first step towards living a more balanced life, breaking your limiting beliefs and moving on by finding your path, opening your heart and being sincere about what's holding you back, what you're tired of and what you really want from your life. It doesn't matter who you are, how old you are, where you live, or what you do for a living – set your expectations for yourself and take the initial step towards your new life!

It doesn't mean you have to quit the job you love – but maybe it will motivate you to make a few changes in how you spend your time at work, how you connect with your fellow workers, or cooperate with your business partners.

After reading this book, you might notice that you won't look at your partner or your children in the same way as you did before because you'll cherish them more.

Perhaps this book will motivate you to treat yourself better and to start taking more time for yourself, to take up a painting class, start a sport activity like running or playing tennis, or start baking and decorating cakes not only for your children, but also for your friends and co-workers.

After reading it, maybe you'll be more willing to open a Facebook page or a blog and share all the beautiful handicrafts, cards, and jewelry you've been hiding in a secret corner of your home. Or perhaps you'll send the movie script you wrote a long time ago to a reputable movie director.

Maybe you'll reorganize how you spend your time and make greater room for the people and activities you enjoy. It doesn't really matter what that is, as long as you enjoy it.

Even if you just decide to take a few hours off, relax and enjoy the book while having a glass of your favorite wine – it's fine. You deserve some time for yourself. Because life's a gift – don't waste it. **So stop chasing weekends and counting days – make every day in your life count.**

17 STEPS TO FIND YOUR **WORK-LIFE BALANCE**

1. Create a vision of your ideal life.
2. Every journey begins with a single step. Make a plan.
3. Set milestones. Reward yourself for reaching each and every one of them.
4. Close the doors that don't lead you to your goal.
5. Let go of the past: treat what's happened to you as a gift.
6. Forgive people who have hurt you and move on.
7. Do what you fear the most.
8. Open yourself up to new ideas, meet new people, and take new opportunities.
9. See good in every situation.
10. Discover your personal mission.
11. Do what makes you happy.
12. Make your own rules.
13. Always believe in yourself.
14. Be grateful. Focus only on the good and positive.
15. Surround yourself with positive people.
16. Spend time wisely. Learn to say NO.
17. Take a deep breath and try. If you fail, try again.

Life is a journey. Have fun on the way; otherwise, you won't be happy at the destination. Stay open to the miracles that are coming your way.

Stop chasing weekends

BONUS:
MESSAGES FROM
WOMEN WHO INSPIRE

IZA LOGIN
KRISTIN ENGVIG
TADEJA BUČAR
ANA LUKNER

BONUS:
MESSAGES FROM
WOMEN WHO INSPIRE

———

People often ask me who my role models are and who inspires me. There are lots of them: I've known some of them for years, but I also believe that an innocent encounter or event that seems to be a coincidence, or just a vague hint by someone, can bring a message that touches you deep down.

I'm delighted to present you with four women who have touched me in a special way: each has inspired me to step onto my new life path, and publishing their stories is my way of saying 'thank you'.

Although at first glance they seem very different, they have much in common. They used to live their lives according to the conventional rules of the world, and then realised that's not what they wanted, that's not how they want to live. They left their well-paid jobs, that were supposed to set them up for life but which, instead, they found to be very unfulfilling.

These are women who couldn't find a culture to fit in with, an environment to encourage them to grow, so they decided to build one themselves.

They found their individuality, their identity and accepted themselves, their special talents and inner beauty.

They change everything they touch, are passionate and curious.

Today, they don't want to be the same as yesterday. They constantly change and seek a better version of themselves, while at the same time bringing life and light to everything they touch.

They are extremely creative and not at all afraid to live and survive. When the going gets tough, they look for new opportunities, bring light and start blossoming in their best possible way.

Guided by responsibility, they are faithful to their values. Their inner beauty shines through them and sheds light on everyone around.

Listen to their stories – they'll remind you of all the good that lies within you. Let them inspire you to start creating the changes you want to see in your life and in the world around you.

IZA LOGIN
WE OURSELVES CREATE THE WORLD WE LIVE IN

———

I admire how easily she weaves her business and spiritual sides together. Iza Login is a computer specialist, who left a pharmaceutical company to join Microsoft, then founded the company Outfit7. With her husband Samo and the team they created the Talking Tom mobile application that has since taken the world by storm. When the company was sold for USD 1 billion, she gave herself the resources to start fulfilling her personal mission: to help humanity and the Earth cope more effectively with the global challenges. She is the leader of a new era: she brings the female principle and ancient wisdoms into the business world. She trusts her intuition, pinpoints her goals and then, with determination, realises them. She does not fear anything as she firmly believes in herself and in the fact that we ourselves create our own reality.

The media most often present Iza Login as the 'mother of Talking Tom' and in the public's eye she is mostly known as a very successful businesswoman. Astrologists have told her she was a very successful businessman already in her past life. She says everything is so simple for her in business, she enjoys it, yet work is not the most important thing in her life. Iza Login is much more than just a successful businesswoman: she is a mother, a wife, a manager, a healer, a motivator, an organiser....

"Being a mom and a wife is what I enjoy most, this matters the most to me. As weird as this may sound, my children are the most important project in life. And I'm not trying to objectify them. Let's take a company project or building a house for example, you finish and move on, whereas children stay for the rest of your life. They are your children for your entire life. If something good happens to them, I feel great but, if anything bad happens, I always ask myself if I have anything to do with that, if I have made a mistake in their upbringing so they have to deal with this in their life. Being a wife and a mother are my two favourite and most responsible roles."

Of course, she is not talking about her being Talking Tom's mother. "This sounds good, yes, the media love it so much. I am very grateful that we did it. I am grateful to every user who played with the app and helped us earn a few cents. I am grateful for the business and the success, but this is not the kind of achievement where you say to yourself – 'wow, I did that really well!' This is simply business, we just make a living with it. My family is what is most important and sacred to me."

I RESPECT ALL PEOPLE

Behind this tender and seemingly fragile appearance hides a headstrong woman who knows exactly what she wants. She mainly sees herself as an organiser and a motivator. "Being a motivator comes naturally to me. When I see someone suffering, I do everything to show them their light and where to move forward." She is really attentive when choosing people to work with, as she is aware that a company's performance depends greatly on how team members relate one to another. She sees her colleagues as people with their own wishes and needs, she makes an effort to understand their goals and help with achieving them. She believes that personal happiness is a major factor of employees' performance and thus also the success of the company they work for.

And respect – a value that has lately become chronically scarce in this world. For her, a person holding an important position or a high title is not a better person than somebody else.

"I respect all people. I respect everybody, but this does not mean that I agree with everyone and I want to spend time with them. I speak my mind, yet I judge no one. Simply because a person holds a position, has power or authority, does not make them more important for me. I talk to you in the same way as I talk to our cleaning lady Borka or the Pope."

I AM NOT AFRAID

Iza enthrals with her leadership approach and attitude to people, colleagues and partners. She tries to understand other people's needs and lets them be what they are, do as they feel and say what they want. What is important for her is that they feel good. She says the key to her success is that she has never feared anything in business.

"One thing is that you do what you want, what you love. Yet we also work to make it through the month. In the past, people had to grow their own food, but today our jobs are more specialised and then we have a trade.

I have never feared I would be unable to survive. A bigger problem for me was that I am very responsible: if I promise something, then I deliver. That was also the reason for my burnout – it pushed me over the edge."

IF I FEEL GOOD, I CAN DO A GOOD JOB

Culture and a good product are both vital for a company's success, Iza believes.

"My husband Samo said the other day that corporate culture is the most important. I don't agree completely with this. Yes, culture is important, but you need a good product first. You can't do anything without a good product. If we just love one another, that alone will not help us succeed."

When she worked for a company whose corporate culture was incompatible with her own, she suffered from burnout within eight months. "No trace of teamwork there, only a bus filled with the best 'propeller heads', where everyone was thinking only about their own career. This killed me. I can't work in such a company. To me, 'human to human' approach is an important thing."

She took the experience she had gained in multinationals, where she managed important projects, into Outfit7 where she was confronted with the challenge of leading a company for the first time. "I said: 'If we have good products and if we are a good team, money will come – we won't have to deal with this'. And they looked at me bewildered. Because that's how it is: if you fly along with your creation, the money comes in, you don't have to bother about it, there's no need to make plans and then adjust them every month. We had plans for our own sake. We always strived to exceed them, to do the best we could."

"Money is just an exchange for energy. If you work with positive energy and enthusiasm, money comes easily. You don't have to focus on that at all."

YOU CAN REACH FOR THE STARS, IF THAT'S CONCEIVABLE

Iza's definition of success is very simple: "If you set yourself a goal and achieve it – that's a success. The goal need not be related to business, for example selling your company for 1 billion dollars. It can be any goal: for instance, you want to climb Mount Triglav – and then you achieve your goal. For me, that's success. But the way you set your goals is also important."

"Your goals must be conceivable. They can go all the way up to the stars, if that's conceivable for you. When we founded Outfit7, our goal was to earn 100 million euros in profit within five years and we actually had this written on the wall. Samo often says: the only person who believed in me was you and nobody else. Because this was so unconceivable to everybody else. Samo is the one who sets ambitious goals, and then I say: 'ok, let's now manifest this. You can set very high goals for yourself, but they must be conceivable. Other people may find them completely unrealistic, that doesn't matter at all. They don't have to be realistic for them – they have to be realistic for me."

Is success the key to happiness for you?

"It's hard for me to say yes and hard to say no", she ponders. "When you achieve a goal, you can be happy, but you can also be happy only partly because you're bothered or saddened by some other thing. I am happy when everybody around me is happy. My husband says he can't be happy if I am not. So there's obviously something to it. I think that the relations we have with other people are the most important factors of happiness. And I guess every person has their own definition of happiness."

EVERYBODY HAS THEIR OWN KRYPTONITE

Even if Iza might seem like a fearless superwoman, at the end of the day she is just a human being. I wondered what lies beneath the surface, what is her 'kryptonite' – what paralyses her, slows her down or stops her.

"I had a very interesting pattern in the past but I wasn't familiar with any technique to deal with it. I was unable to finish anything, I couldn't stick through to the end. In primary school, for example, when we did handicrafts, such as crochet or knitting, I always completed about 80 percent and then, if somebody else around me had already finished and started doing something else,

I would unravel my piece and start something else. And my best friend made herself a woollen vest and a sweater and everything, whereas I went empty handed.

When I studied at university, I realised computer science was not my cup of tea and I wanted to study psychology. And then Samo commented that I was unable to finish anything because I always got tired of it. This hit me to the core. 'What, you're telling me I can't finish anything?'. When somebody pinches you so strongly, you say NO. Since then, I always finish everything I start. These days, I don't even start if I know I won't be able to finish it. And I always persevere. I tell other people the same, for instance those who only have a diploma to finish: come on, make the effort, just a little more and you'll be done. When you finish something, you actually feel relief. But back then, I had no clue how to find the cause, I didn't understand my subconscious mind."

IT IS ONLY WHEN YOU BECOME AWARE OF YOUR LIMITING BELIEFS AND PATTERNS THAT YOU CAN CONFRONT THEM

Given her knowledge about personal growth, the study of astrology and ThetaHealing, plus the vast experience she has gained in her in-depth work with people, Iza could easily be a healer. And I am sure she'd be successful.

When she recognised specific patterns and beliefs in herself, slowing her down or stopping her, she wanted to know why.

"During my research, I found old religious scripts where Jesus said that you are born with two or three knots and that those are the things you have to resolve when you come into this world as a human being.

Well, I have three such root patterns or knots: humiliation, restraint and control. Restraint is the most visible on the outside.

When I have to pack a suitcase, I can do it in five minutes, but I need one hour to prepare myself for it, simply because it involves packing all the necessities into a very limited space. When we moved to Cyprus, we left Slovenia carrying one suitcase each. We bought a holiday bungalow, without a storage room, but with the most beautiful view of the sea. We consciously gave up space for this view. The bungalow was so small that our bedrooms were used as offices, too. And I said to myself that this is only my restraint and that I can handle this, as we have enough space.

Restraint is also part of my life, I am constantly being restricted: for example, I can do this, but I can't do that, this doesn't look fine, that is not right, I'd do it this way.... Anyway, if you're aware of your pattern, you accept it, and then you move forward. And you can release this feeling in half a minute. Restraint is the one I can manage the easiest.

Then there are control and humiliation. If I'm angry, it's like pressing my 'control button', which means there was something I couldn't control and I am angry because something happened or did not happen.

When I am sad, it's my 'humiliation button'. It's not that I feel *I'm not loved, I'm not accepted, I'm not good...* – no, I simply feel humiliated and I'm aware of this feeling. I accept it and let it go. I can move on in a flash. But it can last even for several days – it's my own decision.

These are three patterns I have been able to identify in myself and it's easier for me to live with them. Of course, you can never replace or get rid of them entirely. But you can peel off layer by layer, like an onion. Each layer that is removed brings more pleasure and joy in your life, so I am not worried when it hurts, because I know that it will get much better soon."

WE ARE RESPONSIBLE FOR WHAT HAPPENS IN OUR LIFE

People tend to shift the responsibility for their life, particularly for all the bad things that happen, to other people. Through her conduct, Iza encourages others to become aware of the causes and take responsibility.

"When you confront yourself, you also realise that you yourself are responsible for what is happening in your life. But many people don't want that: it's easier to blame somebody else and pin the responsibility for what is happening on somebody else. Some other person will do something or they must do something to make me feel good. For example, my husband has to change so that I can be happy, and so on. People refuse to take responsibility."

WE ALL HAVE THE POSSIBILITY TO CHOOSE

Every one of us has infinite possibilities in every moment of our life, but it depends exclusively only on us which option we choose. As long as good things come into your life, it's simple. But everybody comes across something that poses a challenge to them. You have to act on it, do something. At that point, you must go beyond yourself and step out of your comfort zone. Iza also talks a lot about this with her colleagues.

"In fact, we always have the possibility to choose. You can't take this away from anyone. But you also can't force anyone to choose anything. You can't force your opinion upon anybody – all you can do is to show them the direction: 'Look, I live like this and do this and I have this experience'. Of course, it doesn't mean that everything is perfect with me. Who says I'm right? Maybe I'm not right, maybe it's all wrong. Maybe, in six months I'll have a totally different view than today. As I can choose at any point in time, I can also change my opinion, if I want to.

We often discuss why someone refuses to 'make a move'. Some people don't hear, don't want to hear, forget, don't understand. Everybody takes what they are willing to take. Even me, I am still touched by certain things and I can feel them very deeply. Then I know I have to take one step further. At such a time, I need someone and I call my friend to help me bring the pain into my awareness. And then I move on because I am not okay with the pain.

To return to the metaphor of the onion: when you feel pain, that's when the onion starts to rot and smells nasty, you have to peel it once again. As soon as you are aware of this, it's no longer difficult. People who work on themselves achieve three times more than those who don't. They are forced into changes by life, as otherwise they could not survive."

ONCE YOU MANIFEST YOUR GOAL, THERE'S NO NEED TO SET THE COURSE

For Iza and Samo Login, Talking Tom was just a means to achieve something more important. Already when establishing Outfit7 they had a clear goal to make a good amount of money, sell the company and invest it to realise their true mission: the non-profit projects they finance with the proceeds of selling their company will be based on technological development aimed at preserving the environment, helping humanity and the Earth.

"Not long ago, we attended the Google Zeitgeist conference in London and they said that if we all lived like we live now, we'd need three planets – that means three Earths – to survive. The most pressing issue facing our world is how to ensure the survival of the many people we already have, whereby the biggest problem is food. The Earth can sustain 4 billion people, and now there are 10 billion of us. These problems can't be solved by awareness-raising campaigns, because there's not enough time. A change in people's habits takes two generations and we don't have this time because, in 40 years, humanity on Earth will come to an end if we don't change radically. We must actually do something.

We'll try to find the solutions and these will have to be better, cheaper and also more attractive. We have commenced with brain research projects to help us understand the feelings and emotions in conjunction with our nutrition."

IZA'S ADVICE TO HER 20-YEAR-YOUNGER SELF

At the end, I asked her what advice she would give to herself if she were 20 years younger.

"I would give myself two pieces of advice: the first is 'start delegating sooner and get help earlier', not only when you can't handle it anymore. If you own a company, you can do it – in my company, I'd certainly delegate some things sooner than I did. In my previous job, I asked for help but I couldn't get it.

The other is that health is the most important thing and that I have to be really aware of this and respect it. Although I know this and I am aware of it, I keep breaking my own rule. I have to remind myself of this constantly. Because every time you go beyond yourself, when you cross that line, it has consequences."

I understand her. I understand what it is like when a challenge sucks you in, especially if you love your work. All limits collapse and you forget about time. You enjoy the ride. And you know you will achieve your goal.

"Even if you don't think you're the best, you are in fact the best. Because, if you're so successful, you're good and you know the ropes. You have to admit this to yourself and that's not arrogance or ego. And if something is missing somewhere, then get the best people out there to help you. If you take on board those who are not the best, you can fail. I love people who are better than me the most. You must be aware that you're not in it for the money, not for the fame, but at that moment your only wish for the project is to succeed."

She gives an example that is very telling about her and proves everything she has just told me about herself. About goals. About responsibilities. About dedication. About passion.

"In Hollywood, we worked on a project where we cooperated with a Slovenian agency, but they couldn't finish their work on time. Then a colleague and myself had to organise the entire event by ourselves. We found a writer in Australia and she stood in by writing a script. We had a good connection in Los Angeles who found us a producer. I took figs, nuts and water and for three weeks moved into the house next door that Sam and I had bought but not yet moved into.

A stylist and Samo travelled with us to Hollywood – we worked our heads off there. When we had shows, I myself undressed Talking Tom and helped him put on another uniform mid show. At the end, after the last show and a press conference, we returned to our hotel at 2 in the morning and I thought I was going to throw up from sheer exhaustion. Well, you see, that kind of stuff…. This was really… – you can't buy such experience.

Well, then my body took its toll. When I cross the line, I do so fully. I should have been wiser in these things, more down-to-earth."

But that is what makes you who you are and why you are successful. If you could change one thing in your life, what would that be?

"I would never study for grades. That for me was the biggest mistake in life, namely throughout my schooling, that is 17 years in total, I studied for grades and now I have to learn everything once again for MYSELF: history, geography…. So much time was wasted and I gained nothing. Okay, you learn languages because you need them, that's for sure. Otherwise, I am more a kinaesthetic type of person, I have to experience things. You know you don't learn only from data but there is this emotional dimension that makes you remember things. For example, I am pleased when someone goes somewhere and then I study everything, where they went, where they stayed…."

Yes, life is our greatest teacher. Every experience and every person crossing our path are our teachers. If only we can open our eyes and listen to them. If only we are willing to accept our challenges and lessons. If only we can look at the life before us with an open heart and carve out our own path, the one we believe leads to a better life for us and our children. And now we know that Iza Login can.

KRISTIN ENGVIG
WE ALL CAN BECOME AGENTS OF POSSIBILITIES

Imagine what it would feel like if you were always seen in the right light.... Imagine transforming the world with all the possibilities that lie within and around you now.... Imagine trusting your inner calling and embarking on a new journey.... Imagine living your dream and inspiring others to live theirs.... Imagine what the world is calling you to do and that this is becoming your destiny....

Using these words, Kristin Engvig welcomes you to WIN, Women's International Networking, the movement she founded 20 years ago to empower and inspire women to speak up and be heard. To have the courage to stand up and break through the glass ceiling at work. To live up to their own dreams, be bold enough to change their own lives and, then, to help other women change theirs.

When I asked her how she'd describe herself, I was surprised to hear her answer.

"I'm an artist. I think like an artist, I function like an artist. WIN was created in my office, at my desk. At the beginning it was a spreadsheet. I had this instinct, I knew what I wanted and I invented it, I created WIN from scratch, like an artist: a framework, a system of work, how to deal with sponsors, speakers, participants. I am an entrepreneur too.

Every year I invent the conference theme: I listen and talk to people, and then come back and start creating it: it's all coming back to me – I'm feeling it, I'm smelling it in a sense. I know that a WIN theme has to empower and inspire the world.

Many people don't see this as a creative process, but I know I'm creating things and that this gives me so much energy. I can also do very repetitive things but, at the end of the day, I get more tired from that. I need to make sure that during the course of the day I spend at least one hour doing something creative, and then the rest of the day I can even do some repetitive things.

I said to my teammate the other day: "I don't need to know everything about what's going on, I just need a report of what's going on." But I want to have a say in the creative process: writing the words, the photos, the videos and the news. I really like that, these are things that give me joy. As I move forward, I think I will spend more time writing, talking, engaging myself in these sorts of creative processes."

UGLY DUCKLING

As a little girl, Kristin had big dreams. She wanted to be a writer, then an actress, a marketing expert, a fashion designer, a teacher, a politician, even an adventure traveller. With an MBA in Economics and an M.Sc. in Business and Marketing, she could have become anything, or all of that. Like many ambitious young women, she decided to take her first career steps in the corporate world, namely at JP Morgan and CityBank. But she wasn't happy there.

"I was good at my job and at the same time I saw many ways for improvements, especially in making the places more inclusive*, but it was tricky. I couldn't tolerate corporate politics and the wasting of time, or unfair things like people being promoted for all the wrong reasons.... I also felt I was underemployed, underutilised, underpaid. Coming from Norway, I didn't understand hierarchies so well, I didn't understand corporate rules, so I talked openly to everyone. But I wasn't heard, I didn't feel significant. Some people can take it – after a while, I just couldn't take it any longer. A bit like millennials today in many countries. I started thinking how to change those organisations, but it was hard.

At that time, I was reading the book Women Who Run with Wolves by Dr Estees. My aunt had given it to me for my 28th birthday. I did not read it immediately but, when I finally did, especially when I got to the chapter about the Ugly Duckling character, I understood that Ugly Duckling was me. I realised I was working in the wrong place and that I could be a swan somewhere else. Just like someone else could probably be a swan in a bank too.... The following day, I quit my job at Citybank."

BUILDING PURPOSEFUL RELATIONSHIPS

After quitting her secure bank job, Kristin was free to try everything she'd always wanted to do professionally. So she started freelancing with various organisations, cooperating with Bocconi University, teaching marketing throughout Eastern Europe and undertaking lots of cross-cultural training around the world. Kristen listened very attentively to the outside world but, most importantly, she also listened to her inner calling, guiding her to take the next step. It would be a bold one.

"For all this time, I was active in a Professional women's association – I loved being with women and talking to them. So I listened to my inner calling and to the voices of many other women and embarked on a new journey: inner and outer. It seemed as if many other women were on the same journey. So I combined my individual journey with what I was hearing outside, from different women, and brought all of this together in my work, a collective journey.
Meanwhile, I also did some acting and creative work. I began studying the creative process, each day undertaking to write 3

of Julia Cameroon's Morning Pages (the artist way). I also began practising yoga and Zen via theatre. Now I know that I would be needing all of these experiences for the day I decided to take the risk and start WIN, so I wouldn't take everything that would happen later personally.

People were not always nice to me, mostly because they didn't understand what I was doing, why and what I wanted to achieve. You must find the courage inside to not be angry, to not take it all personally. I realised that part of change is that, no matter what others think or say about you, you still do what you believe is the right thing for you to do."

A VISION TO CHANGE THE WORLD

In 1997, Kristin established WIN, Women's International Networking, with a view to inspiring women around the world and empowering them to break through and make their voices heard. In the last 20 years, WIN has grown into a global organisation with a strong voice, one that empowers women all around the globe.

WIN's annual conference attracts over 700 women from more than 70 countries. Many conferences have themes, but this one has a vision. Kristin believes that it is only when we share our individual and collective dreams with others that we can accelerate the realisation of those dreams. Many reputable organisations with a global impact as well as individuals support WIN's vision – a vision that has contributed to WIN's community growth and global expansion.

What do you think has been the biggest reason for WIN's community growth and global expansion over the past 20 years?

"I believe it was the joint feeling of WE who will change the world. A deep desire to improve the world, the workplace and ourselves, to share that vision so that others would feel part of it. A truly creative approach to it, waiting for the themes to emerge, without manipulating anything.

WIN was created according to what women had been telling me and what I saw was going on in companies. I have a deep understanding of feminine–masculine values and I'm trying to integrate all of that, to put things together so they work – it's a whole system.

WIN inspires women to step into decision-making roles, advance their careers and excel in business as they lead in an authentic, feminine way. It's a total and 100% commitment to a feminine way. With the transformation around us – a global raising of consciousness and the awareness of our interconnectedness – this all supports our efforts as well as the belief in the authenticity and significance of our contribution.

When I started out in 1997, I was not always understood and, especially in the early ages, more criticised. On the other hand, when companies and individuals became ready for it, we were already there.

It didn't happen overnight – it was an evolution: companies started realising that women are well educated. Women were waking up and didn't want to be treated poorly anymore, they wanted promotions. As women started to speak up, companies started to wake up too, realising that women possess many talents.

WIN proposes a more feminine way of doing things, which also means creating a more conscious business."

SUCCESS IS FINDING YOUR PURPOSE

In a world that mainly measures success by how much money is in one's bank account, magnificent houses or the number of cars parked in front of them, it's refreshing and encouraging to know someone who thinks of success in different terms. Someone whose modesty is reflected not only in the way she thinks and speaks, but also in the way she lives, always putting others before herself. Someone who is actually learning to become more selfish. Not because she needs things, but because it will make her son (and maybe also herself) feel better....

What's your definition of success?

"Success... I find that I'm successful when I can contribute to the evolution of the world, of others and my own life – that is great. Success is if we find our purpose and can contribute to the world with that. Also, having love, family and community is important.

I have not been very successful in traditional terms and have always attempted to live very humbly. I'm perhaps a bit too extreme with that. Lately, though, I have actually been wishing to have greater material success as I realise that is also important; within limits, of course.

So there must be a balance in everything. I think now I will focus on getting a few more things for me in the traditional sense, just because it feels nice and so I can invite people home and my son will feel better. Not that I need to do that to show off, but just to feel good. And, having actually having worked so extremely hard, I suddenly realise that I deserve that.... (LOL)

Being on a journey, we grow and learn and some people go from selfish to selfless, yet others need to go from selfless to actually having a self that also needs things...."

YOUR STRENGTH IS YOUR WEAKNESS

Kristin is a strong woman who has long recognised what was limiting her power. Over the years, she has learnt to recognise her limiting beliefs and negative thought patterns that were holding her back and to transform them into ways that help her move forward in pursuing her mission with even greater confidence and authenticity.

"In the past, I was extremely shy and that was holding me back; I always used WE in much of my writing and creations, and had a hard time saying 'I' until just recently...
I have always wanted harmony and – although for many this represents a NEW way, it needs to be in balance, too. In Zen, we say your strength is your weakness. Generosity is what people like me for, I think, but it's also why I can get myself into trouble...

I was previously in a very violent relationship, forcing me to work a lot on setting my boundaries. I fought hard for both my son and my own life. This involved having to move country and many sad things that required a lot of courage and time to deal with. That was very unfortunate. I dedicate considerable time to helping other women understand the need to stay away from sociopaths, how to get out, and how to help each other. Suddenly, my own story presented itself as a gift."

Have you ever been afraid?

"I am not very afraid – hardly ever. I am stressed though – now that I have so many emails to reply to and WIN faces a risky financial situation. I sometimes have no idea how I will pay the salaries of my staff – but it is not fear; at times I feel overwhelmed and also angry as I think that by now it should be easier to fund women's projects."

I AM DOING THE BEST I CAN

All at once, she is a mother and the 'mother' of an organisation, a business woman, a member of the community, a friend.... She travels a lot, but likes to make lunch appointments and have fun with friends. She is full of life, likes to laugh, has many interests....

How difficult is it to leverage and manage all of your different roles on a daily basis?

"Yes, I feel very much like I'm transitioning into a mature woman these days.... Each day, I'm doing as much as I can of everything. It is just one TOTAL me doing it all – I don't think about it.

I should probably wish that I didn't also have to be the father of my son, but I am doing the best I can. Yet I am lucky as my family have been very supportive. I always try to consciously make time for friends because it is so easy to just work through life, especially with my type of personality and the responsibilities I hold.

Sometimes, being a mother and mothering an organisation – I have to really try hard to ensure I have a social life in order not to become sad. I am such a family and community person and, without them, I'd soon feel very lost – so that is important.

WE ALL ARE AGENTS OF POSSIBILITIES

I admire her: her energy, determination and style. I admire how gracefully, seemingly effortlessly and with style she is developing the WIN network for the purpose of supporting, connecting and inspiring women to live out their dreams, to live up to their full potential.

It's a mission that demands considerable courage and determination as the business world is today still mostly run in a more masculine way, by force, competition and exclusion.
In contrast, WIN supports developing women on the inside, integrating their authenticity, their hearts into business to develop compassionate leadership, with a view to supporting cooperation, diversity and inclusion.

What's the secret source of your motivation, courage and power?

"Well, I am on a journey – a creative one – so I create and wait to see what comes out. I have total trust in what comes my way – and I desire to truly create possibilities. I also do yoga, swim, meditate and write a journal.

I was born optimistic and am lucky in that way, and I'm also lucky that I have had so much energy to be able to do so much. The world needs women's authentic contribution at the moment – it's urgent, so I don't think too much about it, I just carry on."

We live in times where constant change is the only constant. It's a perfect opportunity to stop, build up our awareness, learn to live now, be present in the moment. To start enjoying the path, not simply running towards the final destination. How do you feel about this? Is the world we are living in an opportunity or a threat?

"Yes, I live like that – walk meditation constantly.... We need to enhance our awareness and move forward in an integrated fashion – be it along the path and by growing, transforming... uplifting and including people. The world is an opportunity and we need to include the many who feel left out and fearful right now.... In creating a world that works for all – we certainly have many opportunities...."

What advice would you give to a 20-year-younger Kristin?

"To be less shy and speak up more. To trust in yourself and that the way you think and see the world is in fact really great. Don't listen so much to criticism as I did in the early part of my journey.... Always have other sensitive people around you and protect your-self from those who are not. Spend time alone more often to recu-perate.

Think a little more about yourself: speak up quicker when things are not ok as we all can run into difficult situations. And simply to continue having fun.

I am happy with the many things that I have done and, despite some losses along the way, I'm grateful for those because they have also helped me to grow.

If you could change one thing about your life, what would that be?

"I would give myself greater freedom to write, create and reach more people with this uplifting and transformative proposal of mine…."

"The time when a woman had to fit in, search for approval and sacrifice her path is coming to an end. Sure, for most of us the journey is long, and yet it is as if women today can no longer be held back and real authenticity is coming through. As humans, we still doubt ourselves and wonder whether we are good enough and even worthy of the possibilities coming our way. That is why we collaborate, we come together to stand for and with each other, and to liven each other up. Do not forget that."

We are all able to become agents of possibility, says Kristin. So whether you're a leader at the top of a world power impacting global change, the manager of a corner office wishing to make improvements, or a woman chasing her own dreams and setting her own boundaries, the time has come to speak up. The time is ripe for us to break through and lead the way as global, authentic and feminine leaders. Every one of us can make a difference in our own little world and, by that, create new opportunities for both ourselves and others.

TADEJA BUČAR
WE NEED TO ACCEPT WHO WE REALLY ARE

———

A smiling face. A creative mastermind concealed in the body of a kind, heartfelt, warm woman full of positive energy and sparkling spirit. We've known each other for years, after having worked together at the same company. She was the shining star of my team: multitalented, always questioning the status quo and searching for new, fresh ideas and solutions. I guess that's one reason she's never really tried to fit into the world of big advertising agencies, even though she might have had a great career in the industry. However, she just couldn't find enough motivation in her surroundings, where she often found herself in conflict with her true values. So she created her own world, one in which she could grow personally, feed her creative hunger and simultaneously support the community.

We've known each other for years: you're a wonderful person, a great storyteller, excellent copywriter, I could go on and on… but, how would you introduce yourself to someone you are meeting for the first time?

"My mojo is creativity and to be creative and to be part of a creative process."

I'm not surprised to hear the word "creative"… /laughs/ But what did you dream of becoming as a little girl? You know, girls dream of becoming teachers, hairdressers, doctors, maybe astronauts? What was on your mind?

"Not that I am aware of anything specific. But what I do remember is that I was always excited about exploring and discovering stuff, and spent lots of time in my own fantasy world, making things and stories up. I was immensely attracted to the Indiana Jones, BMX Bandits and Karate Kid movies. And I loved playing with Lego."

PROVOKING THE STATUS QUO

What's recently been keeping you up at night, what's your WHY? Why do you do what you do?

"For some time, I thought I needed to fix stuff because nobody else was doing it. I almost killed myself twice in recent years before it became clear that the race is long and we might not live long enough to see the change (although it's already here and we know it and feel it). I get nervous when hearing a sentence of resignation like: "It's how it is". Of course, some things are just as they are, like we are born and then we die but, apart from this, everything can change for the better. Deep down inside, I like to be a showcase of possibilities. I like to inspire people by revealing different angles, I like to provoke the status quo.

The bottom line: my WHY lies in the belief that by being an example of how you live and demonstrating your attitude, you actually provide the strongest example of how you think the world should be like, and that this is the most you can do about things that are broken.

Also, I don't want to be in the hands of others, so I keep creating my own flow. I just want to feel free."

So to sum up: to serve as an example and thereby show others new directions, open up new ways of looking at things,

new opportunities… like PUNKT for example. Where did you get the inspiration for PUNKT, the alternative, underground development agency, as you call it? How did it start?

"It all started when I first entered the world of freelancing in 2000 and discovered the new perspective of time. Becoming a freelancer completely changed my perception of time. I realised there is no difference between Wednesday or Sunday. They are both days. And it's up to me how I organise and manage these days, time. So I can go for a hike on Tuesday when the weather is great and I can work all day long on Saturday as the only thing that's important is that the job is done.

At that time, there were not many freelancers in Slovenia, not many people with whom I could share a freelance lifestyle. It was pretty frustrating sometimes, and also boring. So I ended up moving to Berlin where my heart started soaring because it was there I found a whole new world, filled with freelancers, co-working spaces and endless bunches of people leading lives beyond 9 to 5 jobs. What a relief! And so that's where the inspiration for PUNKT comes from: Berlin. The city that opened my eyes to how creativity can start growing right from out of a graveyard of empty factories and other industrial spaces, so similar to my own hometown.

PUNKT is a lab for creative industries that is organised as a co-working space and a community of creatives from various professions and backgrounds, joined together by the same values and ideas. It is designed as a platform to provide an environment for work, to hang out and to educate for freelancers, activists, entrepreneurs, artists, doers and thinkers. It assures a flexible space and a lively community that wants to work together or change something for the better. It's a space that exists to support creativity and what emerges from it when people with shared values work together."

Stop chasing weekends

REVIVING THE COMMUNITY

In a period when the average person is occupied with the 'strings and arrows' of their own lives, she devotes her attention to social entrepreneurship initiatives, thinking about reviving the community by developing and/or supporting projects with a positive social impact. Not just in words, but by actually creating new opportunities in places that have long been forgotten by government institutions or society, creating new employment opportunities especially for young people, and so on. Like the idea of strategically revitalising empty, abandoned spaces in industrial areas that was first trialled in her hometown, and then in 2015 won the award for Best Entrepreneurship Idea with a Social Impact in Central and Eastern Europe in the Startery programme.

Can you tell us more about Post-Apokalypsa?

"The idea of Post-Apokalypsa is to help solve the huge problem of empty, abandoned spaces in ghost towns that suffer from post-industrial symptoms. We were looking at empty spaces in our hometown that once were the cathedrals of a flourishing industry and are today crumbling in front of our eyes in every step we take. We asked ourselves what we could do with these spaces, how we could create new purposes for them and breathe new life into them. And without any money. So we developed an interactive field game, a kind of a treasure hunt or an outdoor escape room that takes place in and around those empty spaces. It is played in teams, only using one's imagination.

The potential is enormous. As many post-industrial places as there are in the world, there are that many fields for playing Post-Apokalypsa. This project is on hold at the moment since it requires much greater resources than we can provide. It's a big open wound."

A wound that will eventually heal when more individuals start thinking not only about themselves, but also about how they can contribute to developing the consciousness of individuals and society.

LEARNING TO LET GO

Today success is often measured by what you have and not by who you are…. What's your definition of success?

"To be the master of managing your time, to ensure that it's up to you how you're going to spend your moments. For me, that means not spending time on useless stuff, boring people, doing things I don't believe in or which don't contribute anything meaningful. The ultimate success is to be surrounded by people you love, you're inspired or impressed by, and with whom you spend most of your time. Every day."

I love it, I completely agree. If only we didn't have all those inner voices and beliefs hindering us from doing what we really love and believe in. What's your kryptonite? Which beliefs have been most limiting and what's your way of facing them?

"Pursuing perfection. Inner criticism. Being a good girl. Being over-responsible and an over-doer at work. I am still dealing with all of these….

Becoming aware of the kryptonite was the first step. Observing it the next time and thereafter knowing how to recognise it when it appears, then getting to know its behaviour, to understand it. And then to say, ok, yes, you're here, but now I have to let go of you. I think I've learned to let things go. I'm still learning when to let the kryptonite go."

Have you ever been afraid? Ever had any fears?

"Of course. Fear of not doing things correctly. Fear of making mistakes. Fear of disappointing others. Fear of being rejected. Fear of not being good enough. Fear of being loved for what I am not. I'm still learning."

Yes, life is all about learning. We learn from other people, we learn from books, but above all, we learn from our own mistakes and failures.

ACCEPT WHO YOU ARE

By playing different roles in life – you're a daughter, a partner, a friend, a community leader, a co-worker…. How do you manage to remain YOU in all of these various situations, how to remain yourself?

"Just be true. These are only the roles we play, but you are you. All you have to do is to be true. The hardest thing with this, I guess, is to accept yourself. It's not about finding yourself. It is about accepting who you really are and having the courage to do that. But, of course, you are creating yourself and who you are in every single moment. Who you are is who you want to be. Practice mindfulness and awareness, respect and always be kind to people. Apart from idiots. Walk away from them!"

So what's your definition of happiness?

"To feel freedom, to be the light, to be calm with yourself, and to be playful. To be aware of the people who love you, to have someone you can be stupid and laugh out loudly with, and to know how to channel or accept pain."

Most people fear change, whereas you help to create it. What are you dreaming about today?

"Travelling around the world in a sailing boat for the next decade, living a life without an intense schedule, and being able to pack all of my life's possessions into one big backpack. Ok, perhaps into two. No, into one. It has to be one!"

Wow, you totally surprised me with this – I love the perspective though. Hmm, actually you opened some new horizons for me, thanks. /laughs/ But aren't we all constantly sailing through our lives? Sometimes the weather is nice, then clouds appear from out of nowhere, even storms…. How do you stay in contact with yourself amid this rapid pace of modern life?

"By trying to be mindful and aware, knowing how and when to step out to see the big picture. Spending time in silence and solitude, being an observer. Crying. Letting things go. My nearest and dearest also act as some sort of benchmark. In addition, writing makes me who I am and keeps me tuned in. I need to write more, again. I promise."

What advice would you give to a 20-year-younger Tadeja?

"Travel, babe, travel more, write babe, write much, much more and please, oh, please, stop worrying!"

If you could change one thing about your life, what would that be?

"I would have started travelling and living abroad much earlier. Also, I wouldn't be so harsh on my body. Like opening bottles with my teeth, and losing and gaining weight as if I am an accordion."

Tadeja, I can easily imagine you as a little girl, playing with your Lego somewhere in the small industrial town of Trbovlje, boldly constructing your dream world. Maybe that was also the time you started to realise you're the creator of your own future. That you're free to do things your way, how you want to. To live the way that seems right to you. To be true to yourself.

I guess the little Tadeja had no idea she would grow up to become someone who others look up to, respect and admire for who she is and for what she's done – for her friends, her clients, and the community. Today, Tadeja knows that our lives start changing the moment we accept ourselves and who we are, when we start being as nice to ourselves as we are to others.

So if I were the mayor of a town where she had come to moor her sailboat on her travels around the world, I'd run down to the harbour to meet with and talk to her and harness her wisdom when constructing a new future for me and for the community.

ANA LUKNER
WE ARE ALL TRUHOMA

I remember the first time I heard of her. It was just before Christmas, when everybody was busy buying presents for their loved ones. All of a sudden, there was this beautiful young woman, telling us to save some of the money we would have otherwise spent on presents, and buy food instead. Food that would feed hungry families and bring smiles to their faces. Food was going to be their Christmas present. It touched my heart. Of course I responded. And so did others. Soon people all over Slovenia were gathering and bringing food for Ana's little star – the charity she founded to support the noble cause. Ana gave us all a powerful message: if you want to change the world and make it a better place, you have to serve as an example first.

At 18, this young talented tennis player got a scholarship and moved to California. She studied at San Jose State University, majoring in international business, and later, went on to receive her MBA, majoring in marketing. After returning to Slovenia, she began working in a large pharmaceutical company, but soon realized that the environment wasn't supportive enough for her to live up to her potential. So she left and started her own business. Even then, she already had a clear vision of her life, one that hasn't changed until today.

Ana, how would you introduce yourself to someone that you meet for the very first time?

"I am Ana, living my vision, changing this world to be a better place, inspire people to reach their highest potential."

Was this something you've dreamt of already as a little girl?

"I was always dreaming of doing many different things through which I could connect and unite people, and make this world a better place. I was raised by great parents with unconditional love. They taught me that you should always help others. So, when I was 4 years old, I was running around saying that I will have my own charity."

ANA'S LITTLE STAR WITH LARGE IMPACT

And so it happened. It all started in 2010, when invitations to her birthday party she sent to her friends included an appeal not to buy her any presents, but instead, to bring some food they would later give to people in need. With the food they collected, they fed 37 families.

But it was so much more than a single action. It was the start of Anina zvezdica - Ana's little star, a non-profit organization that would in years to follow collect more food than any other charity in the country, now feeding more than 100,000 hungry families. And all this fueled only through the good will and empathy of people, who like Ana, have an extreme sense of generosity and empathy.

By providing food, Ana's little star charity brings happiness to thousands of families every year and mobilizes hundreds of volunteers all around the country. Today it is also supported by many companies, employees, schools and kindergartens, etc. However, this didn't happen overnight. One of the important factors of success was that the entire campaign was completely transparent and implemented without any funds. I guess that was one of the reasons that it touched the hearts of so many people.

"Ana's Little Star (Anina zvezdica) is our free time and done completely without money and, therefore, it is transparent. No hidden motives or agenda. Therefore, people simply feel it and want to be a part of it. They feel connected, they feel love and they want to help. Moreover, I knew from the beginning that Ana's Little Star would be successful since we are all born good and pure. Sometimes we just need someone or something to awaken us. I believe in the good of people."

Ana mobilized people all over the country, resulting in Ana's little star becoming the biggest, transparent non-profit organization in Slovenia. In 2012 the Slovenian national newspaper named her National Person of the Year, and in 2013 she was named National Woman of the Year by a respected Slovenian national lifestyle magazine. Among her top honors, even the Slovenian President Borut Pahor recognized Ana for her outstanding achievement in philanthropy and ethical leadership. Her work didn't go by unnoticed elsewhere either in 2015 she received the Ethics & Social Responsibility award from the European Union Association.

But what I think is the greatest reward and most important for Ana: gratitude from all the people, she helped by starting her initiative.

WE NEED TO BE OUR OWN INSPIRATION

Today, Ana shares her story as an inspirational speaker, often addressing large audiences, including TEDx and audiences in the U.S. and throughout Europe to share insights into business success and philanthropic leadership. In her speech, she talks about TruHoMa, the concept of Truth and Honesty in business, through "True and Honest" Marketing, Management and Mankind.

"The title of my inspirational speech is 'Inspiration Is You'. I tell my story and touch many different aspects, experiences and beliefs. If you do not live the raw life and embrace everything that comes with it, especially hard experience (which in the end always turns out to be good for something), you are not living at all. And for that, you need to be TruHoMa (True and Honest Mankind). It is our duty to be true and honest and to dig deep into ourselves to become who we really are. And for that, we need to be our own biggest inspiration. Once you realize that, once you find the inspiration within you, you begin flying and really living your life to your fullest potential. This is my message. I give this message, this inspiration to people ... and miracles happen. When we turn off our ego, there is only love ... and love is the answer for everything. Love is being TruHoMa."

Why do you do all this in the first place?

"I simply feel it. I live and do my dream, my vision. I feel and know that this is why I was put on this planet."

In one of her talks, Ana said that life's ups and downs are necessary so we can discover our real values, our true potential and realize who we really are. But still, even when we do so, sometimes we get stuck and search for an external inspiration. I was curious to hear what's been driving her.

"I am my own biggest inspiration. I realized a long time ago that my greatest source of power is within me. It is pure love. Once you accept who you really are, the whole truth, only love is left ... no more ego. Then, everything else is pretty simple. The unconditional love that I receive from and see in my parents is something that gives me much fuel as well."

Were you ever afraid? At all?

"When I was young, I used to be afraid of death. But I learned that being afraid is acting out of ego. I am not afraid of anything. I simply trust that everything is as it should be as long as I am me."

Most of the time, we ourselves can be our biggest limitations: our limiting beliefs, thought patterns… What were yours and how did you deal with them?

"I used to care a lot about what other people said or thought of me. I allowed the outside world to affect me. And soon I realized that it didn't matter. What matters is the fact that I feel good in my skin and that I feel free and that I can live my vision. And getting to this point is not easy it takes constant practice."

Besides being a philanthropist, Ana is also a successful entrepreneur; she runs her own business and is also a the Managing Director of ABC Silicon Valley.

What's your definition of success?

"For me, success is having family and friends, being content with oneself and above all, giving to others. It is giving, sharing love. That is true success for me. Everything else   career success eventually comes when you work hard."

I TRUST MY INTUITION

Not so long ago, she had so many obligations she hardly took time for herself. But that changed.

"I now take Ana time because only in that way can I maintain the Ana spirit and vision. Everybody needs to stop, take time and simply breathe. In that way you are fully connected."

In this fast pace of life, how do you maintain contact with yourself?

"I work on so many different things and am surrounded with so many people, but I make sure to have alone time. I love it. It is like a reset and I usually do one of several things: running, hiking, cooking, cleaning ... but mostly I love to just sit and observe. I love to spend time in nature ... and think. During these moments, I am extremely connected with myself, totally calm ... and during this moments, I see an even clearer vision of my life ... I trust my intuition."

What are you dreaming of today?

"Nothing big. Just simply of being me, doing great things, inspiring people, making changes and being with my family, and also to have family of my own ..... to get married really soon."

What advice would you give to a 10 year younger version of you?

"To be who you really are, to listen to your intuition and to do what you think you are here for."

If you could change one thing about your life, what would it be?

"Honestly, I am grateful for everything just the way it is."

Ana believes that everybody in this world can become a TRUE and HONEST person: if we have a true and honest mind, we can do miracles. We just need to be in sync with ourselves, with who we really are and apply that into everything we do.

We don't need money to become true and honest person ... we just need awareness and devotion. If we are true and honest in what we do, we can all be winners and give our share to true and honest mankind. We're all TRUHOMA.

AFTERWORD

Dear reader,

yes, it's that simple: **work-life balance is all about having a MEANINGFUL life!**

Don't allow the pressure of what's going on around you or what other people think to put you off track. We can't always control external circumstances, but we can always choose how we react to them.

Have the confidence and the power to react so that you remain true to yourself, your beliefs and values and, thereby, sustain your inner balance.

Since the book first came out in sLOVEnia, a small country on the sunny side of the Alps in Europe, it has touched the hearts of thousands of women, who in turn are spreading the message and, by that, creating a community of women who want more from their lives. I'm so grateful for this.

I've been invited to companies and events to share the message in inspirational talks and workshops, empowering people to become more proactive, to find their work-life balance and win their lives back.

And, yes, this book has not only changed the lives of many readers, it has also changed my life and turned it upside down. I didn't expect it, but I accepted it. I'm still learning to live with it, though. I'm grateful for all the opportunities that have come my way, and am embracing everything that still awaits me.

Because life is a journey. I know that without fun along the way, I won't be happy at the destination.

With love,

Maja

CHALLENGE FOR YOU:

WHAT CAN YOU DO TO CHANGE THE LIVES OF PEOPLE ARO-UND YOU?

DELIGHTED ABOUT THE BOOK? **SPREAD THE LOVE!**

POST YOUR REVIEW, your favourite quote or/and a photo of the book on your social media profile (Facebook, Twitter, Instagram, Linkedin, ...)

SHARE YOUR STORY OR OPINION:
write to us at info@stopchasingweekends.com

GIVE THE BOOK as a gift to your friend, daughter or colleague at work to show you believe in her and are supporting her in every step of her journey to build the life she's always dreamed of.

Together, we can create a better future for us all!

GET **IN TOUCH**

FOLLOW US: facebook.com/stopchasingweekends
www.stopchasingweekends.com/blog

ORDER BOOK ONLINE: www.stopchasingweekends.com

INSPIRE YOUR AUDIENCE OR EMPLOYEES:
speaking@stopchasingweekends.com

> Inspirational talks & workshops and team buildings for enterprises, organisations, events or communities; topics:

STOP CHASING WEEKENDS – how to find work-life balance, without trading one for the other, and win your life back by creating a sustainable change while living a meaningful life

STOP CHASING A DREAM JOB – how to dismantle internal hurdles, build a strong personal brand and move ahead in your career

STOP CHASING HAPPINESS – discover your personal mission, face your fears and create a more meaningful life

REQUESTS FOR INTERVIEWS: pr@stopchasingweekends.com

FEEDBACK OR QUESTIONS: info@stopchasingweekends.com

www.stopchasingweekends.com

ACKNOWLEDGEMENTS

—

FROM THE BOTTOM OF MY HEART, I'D LIKE TO THANK:

- my parents: my mum for always being there for me and my dad for teaching me to always follow my dreams;
- my Aco, the love of my life and my best friend, for loving and supporting me, always encouraging me to go that extra step and make it happen;
- my children Luna and Luka for giving me unconditional love and showing me how I can become a better person every day;
- Maka, Mišo, and Rok for support at all times;
- Mateja and Darko for dragging me out of the flat on that cold New Year's Eve;
- my good friends, who I know I can always turn to;
- my dear friend Enver, who made my greatest wish come true;
- Sandi and Livija for giving me a lifetime opportunity to learn and grow professionally;
- my beautiful Nia dancers for restoring the joy in me;
- dear Sonja for leading with questions, motivation, and opening new perspectives;
- the first readers: Barbara, Darja, Livija, Mateja, Nives, Sonja, and Tadeja – your feedback was priceless and a sign that I was on the right way;
- dear Iza, Kristin, Tadeja and Ana for sharing their inspiring stories;
- every single person who has crossed my path because I know my journey wouldn't have been the same without you; and
- the Universe for giving me the gift to write and empower people.